Homesick for God

FULFILLING OUR DEEPEST LONGING FOR SPIRITUAL REUNION

JOEL G. GREGORY

NELSON IGNITE
A Division of Thomas Nelson Publishers
Since 1798

www.thomasnelson.com

Dedicated
to the people of

Travis Avenue Baptist Church,

who help many
come home to God.

Homesick for God

Copyright © 1990 by Word, Inc.

Unless otherwise indicated, all Scripture quotations are from the New International Version of the Bible, copyright © 1973, 1978, 1984 by the International Bible Society. Used by permission of Zondervan Bible Publishers. Those marked NKJV are from the New King James Version . Those marked KJV are from the Authorized King James Version.

Library of Congress Cataloging-in-Publication Data

Gregory, Joel C., 1948–
  Homesick for God : fulfilling our deepest longing for spiritual
reunion / Joel C. Gregory.
    p.   cm.
  ISBN 0-8499-9028-9
    1. Spiritual life—Baptist authors.   2. Reunions—Religious aspects—
Christianity.   I. Title.
mi4501.2.G749   1990
248.2'5—dc20   90–35634
                                                                        CIP

012349 AGF 987654321
Printed in the United States of America

Contents

Contents

iii

Introduction

The photograph, in black and white, shows a young girl, her shoulder-length blond hair parted down the center and pulled back behind her ears. Her eyes, set low beneath a high forehead, are light in color and widely spaced. Her smile reveals metal braces across upper teeth. *This is a very pretty child,* you think. Then you notice the words beside the photograph: "Missing Person."

A million children are reported missing each year. Many are teen-age runaways. This tragedy of modern society seems symbolic of an even more tragic situation in our spiritual life. Many children of God have run away from home. They have turned away from the Father, away from the warmth of His presence, away from the comforting relief of His grace.

There is a sadness in this life away from God. But there is also hope. There is good news, even there: God wants these runaways to come back. He searches for them, beckons to them, welcomes them back into the protecting embrace of His everlasting arms.

If you are living away from God—no matter how far you have wandered, no matter how long you've been gone— you can come home. Perhaps, reading this book, you will find the encouragement you need to turn back to the Lord Jesus. And then, with God's help, you'll have the strength to stay, running away no more.

Are you homesick for God? Are you a runaway from the Father? You can come home to Him. To begin, stop running— and turn around. . . .

Part I

Turning Away
from God

Then Jesus told them this parable: "Suppose one of you has a hundred sheep and loses one of them. Does he not leave the ninety-nine in the open country and go after the lost sheep until he finds it? And when he finds it, he joyfully puts it on his shoulders and goes home. Then he calls his friends and neighbors together and says, 'Rejoice with me; I have found my lost sheep.' I tell you that in the same way there will be more rejoicing in heaven over one sinner who repents than over ninety-nine righteous persons who do not need to repent.

"Or suppose a woman has ten silver coins and loses one. Does she not light a lamp, sweep the house and search carefully until she finds it? And when she finds it, she calls her friends and neighbors together and says, 'Rejoice with me; I have found my lost coin.' In the same way, I tell you, there is rejoicing in the presence of the angels of God over one sinner who repents."

Luke 15:3–10

1

God Looks for Those Who Leave

On a warm afternoon in September 1982 Patsy Wheat left her two-year-old son Jay playing in the carport with his eight-year-old sister and five-year-old brother. Her husband Harold, a long-distance trucker, wasn't due home until later that night. She set her oven timer for ten minutes, a trick to remind her to check the children. When the timer sounded ten minutes later, she went to check where the children were playing.

Jay was gone. The two older children hadn't noticed that he had somehow disappeared. Six and a half acres of lawn and woods surrounded their Bedford, Virginia home. But Patsy's first concern was the four-lane highway near the home, so she raced there. She did not see little Jay.

Trying to stifle fears of kidnapping, she first called the state police. Then she called the Bedford County sheriff's office. Within thirty minutes, patrol cars, rescue trucks, and a hundred people had gathered on her lawn to help with the search. By nine o'clock that night, a helicopter and a pair of bloodhounds had both proved ineffective.

When her husband arrived at 11 P.M., hundreds of volunteers were involved in the fruitless search, walking hand in hand through the woods. Some had been cut by briars; some had fallen down in exhaustion. The temperature was down to 65 degrees. But the volunteers continued their search in the bramble- and briar-laden area, thinking of the barefooted little boy wearing only shorts and a T-shirt.

Only one possibility remained. A slight, gray-headed woman was summoned with an air-scenting German shepherd. At 4:30 A.M. the dog picked up a scent, ran up a mountainside, and barked wildly. When rescuers reached the dog, it was licking little Jay, whose bleeding feet were caught in briars.

At the bottom of the mountain, a sea of people cheered with joy. A little boy lost was found. But greatest of all was the joy of Patsy Wheat. There is joy in finding one who is lost. (Patsy Wheat, "Please Find My Son," *Redbook*, May 1985, pp. 24, 260)

Jesus explained that such joy in finding the lost is the most distinctive characteristic of God Himself. In Luke 15 Jesus gave to all the ages this description of His Father: More than anything else, God wants to find whose who are lost. If you have gone away from God, He wants you to come back.

What else is God like? Jesus gave these pictures: He is like a shepherd who will leave the flock of a hundred sheep to find the one that is lost. He is like a woman who will turn over her house to find one lost coin, and like a father who will wait hopefully for the return of the son who has left. God seeks those who are lost, and His greatest joy is their recovery. When you have gone away from God, He gets no pleasure out of the emptiness, alienation, and lostness you experience.

In the three stories in Luke 15, Jesus revealed the depths of God's heart. God simply wants you to come back. Whatever the reason you have gone away, God wants you to come

4

home. These word pictures show how much He longs for your return.

JESUS AND THE LOST

Jesus said, "The Son of Man came to seek and to save what was lost" (Luke 19:10). With invisible chains, He drew the lost toward Him. Those labeled irreligious were drawn to Him as if to a magnet.

The greatest chapter of Jesus' parables begins with the statement, "Now the tax collectors and sinners were all gathering around to hear him." The mark of Jesus' ministry was His attractiveness to the abhorrent, repulsive, despised, and branded of His age. These are presented as two different groups: tax collectors and sinners. "Tax collectors" referred to the most despised Jews of them all. The Roman Empire did not collect its own taxes. It sold franchises for tax collection, and the Jews who bought the franchises were considered by their fellow Jews as traitors to God and country—both blasphemous and unpatriotic. "Sinners" referred not just to those who committed sins, but also to certain occupations of people—shepherds, tanners, and people who could not keep the Pharisees' legalistic interpretations of the Ten Commandments. (And remember, the Pharisees had subdivided the Ten Commandments into 613 manmade rules. Most of the people could not even remember them, no less keep them!)

You may have grown up learning who the tax collectors, or publicans, were in the New Testament. What you may not understand, though, is the shock value those characters carried during Jesus' day.

To explain, suppose your church began to attract only those people who were on parole from the state penitentiary, or those out on bond from the county jail. Along with them, suppose your church attracted some of the more affluent con men, extortionists, and ripoff artists in your area, plus slum

5

landlords and massage parlor hostesses. Now suppose at the same time the religious establishment of the city openly rejected your church and condemned its direction.

The scribes and Pharisees were repelled by Jesus. The scribes were the interpreters of the law—professional religionists. The Pharisees were a layman's league of never more than six thousand men. They were the guardians of personal piety and purity. When they saw the kind of crowd attracted to Jesus, the Bible says they "murmured." The word suggests a quiet complaint continually and habitually whispered to one another. One can almost hear the disdain in their words: "This man actually welcomes these people." They could not imagine Him even tolerating such a crowd. But their ultimate sneer was saved for another habit of Jesus: He actually sat down and ate with them.

If you could imagine all this, you would understand the situation in the ministry of Jesus Christ. Lost people continually came to Him. And they came more and more as His ministry progressed. They were not groupies seeking to be close to a great man. They really knew that He cared for them. In this regard, Jesus stands unique among all biblical figures. The Jewish scholar Claude Montefiore states that no one whose life was recorded in the Old Testament or other Jewish writings had this effect on lost people. They simply wanted to be near Him.

Do you feel far away from God? Have your circumstances created a sense of alienation from your spiritual home? This is not a secondary question on the periphery of spiritual life. The central aspect of Jesus' ministry was to appeal to those who were lost. Even today, Jesus wants you to come back.

Tennessee Williams's family moved to a city during the famous playwright's childhood where he and his younger sister and wanted to join a church's choir. Because of their less-than-perfect social situation, they were made to feel like untouchables. He never went back to church. One wonders what the outcome would have been if his talents had been captured for the church rather than the world. What if the man with the vivid dramatic imagination to write *Streetcar Named Desire,* and *Cat on a Hot Tin Roof* had used his creative genius for the kingdom of God?

Jesus wants us to understand that He represents God in His search for the lost. Jesus is like this. Those who follow Him should be like this, too.

THE REALITY OF LOSTNESS

Jesus did not denounce His detractors with anger. He reasoned with them from common experience, reminding them they would leave the flock to find one lost sheep. By arguing from the lesser to the greater, He pointed out, shouldn't He turn aside to find lost human beings? If a peasant woman would turn her house upside down to find a missing coin, should He not turn the accepted order of things upside down to find a lost person?

Just what did Jesus mean when He described being lost? Again, He gives word pictures to help us understand the reality of lostness. For example, a sheep is lost through heedlessness. It does not willfully separate from the flock. A stone that falls, a snake that crawls, or a gap in a pasture wall may frighten or beckon a sheep away from the flock. The sheep is heedless, stupid, or unwary. A flock of one hundred sheep was an average size flock in Jesus' time. One can picture the shepherd in the evening, counting the sheep before closing them into the pen—and then recounting again: ninety-nine. Every Pharisee hearing the story knew that a Hebrew shepherd would search for one missing sheep.

Jesus wants you to understand that God seeks people even when they are lost through their own stupidity, or heedlessness, or carelessness. A teen-ager experiments with drugs for the first time and is hooked. A married person flirts with passion and in a sudden gust of unexpected lust is swept into a situation never expected. A debt-ridden employee takes money from the till, expecting to pay it back. Such people are

7

heedless and stupid like a sheep—but Jesus says God seeks them anyway.

A coin, on the other hand, is lost through carelessness. In the parable of the lost coin, Jesus continued the same lesson, but with several contrasts. These contrasts in the parables are between a man and a woman, relative affluence and poverty, outdoors and indoors, a living sheep and an inanimate coin. A sheep is lost through its own stupidity. A coin is lost through no fault of its own. The coin in question was a Greek drachma, the equivalent of a Roman denarius, which was the wage for one day's labor. It was one-tenth of what this woman had. But it meant more than that to her.

Women of that generation may have worn a circlet of ten coins on their foreheads. This would have been the woman's dowry, a sacred gift related to her marriage—and all that she had of her own. The ornament of beauty was marred by the loss of one coin—as was her very person.

Forty-two percent of American people claim to attend church every week. What of the 50 percent who never go, who are living away from God? What of the children in those families who, through no fault of their own, never hear a word about God, Christ, values, commandments, Bible stories, spiritual truths, or anything related to reverence or spiritual life? Does God seek them? Does the Great Shepherd's heart long for them? Jesus says "Yes."

Both the parable of the lost sheep and the parable of the lost coin point out the value to God of "the one." Whether it's one out of ten or one out of one hundred, God values the one. In contrast, much of our lives today are lived in a suffocating depersonalization, as shown by the names we have applied to decades during the past fifty years:

In the 1940s Franklin Roosevelt spoke of a generation that had a "rendezvous with destiny."

In the 1950s we were called the Silent Generation, and David Reisman spoke of the lonely crowd who developed values by looking at others.

8

Then came the Now Generation of the 1960s, sure of itself and wanting to work its will on others.

The 1970s was the Me Generation, living largely for self-fulfillment and ego gratification.

The 1980s has been called the Uncaring Generation.

Vance Packard called us a nation of strangers. Louise Bernikow calls loneliness an American epidemic. AT&T urges us to reach out and touch someone. Life has become privatized. We do not even know what other people are here for any more. The television, computer, and bank-teller machine eliminate the need for others.

Five billion people now occupy this planet. But this planet is a speck in the Milky Way, 100,000 light-years across. The Milky Way is one galaxy among ten billion other galaxies. The largest known object in the universe is galaxy 3C-236 in Leo Minor, which is 18.6 million lightyears across. In light of this, it makes all the difference whether God really cares for the one, the individual, the single, solitary person. Jesus Christ dares to say that the God who created it all searches that universe for "the one." And nothing else brings Him the joy He feels at finding that lost person. He wants you to come back.

SEARCHING FOR THOSE WHO LEAVE

Rescue requires thoroughness. When the shepherd searches for the one sheep that is lost, he does not abandon the ninety-nine. He leaves them safely in the pen, with other undershepherds standing watch. But the shepherd's passion is to find the one that is lost. One can picture the shepherd seeking through crags and dunes for the lost sheep. Remember, the shepherd stands for God. God does not have to leave His own found ones to make the search. But the search is His passion.

The story of the lost coin also recalls the thoroughness of the search. The woman lived in a typical Palestinian peasant's house with no windows and a low door. Her home was so dark she had to light a candle for the search even during the day.

She used a broom of brush to jostle the coin in order to hear its tinkle against the barren floor. This turned the house upside down. Furniture turned over, dust raised, household in a mess—everything to find the coin.

For two days in October 1987 the whole world was gripped by the drama of "the one." Even as an Iranian missile hit an American-flagged tanker and the Dow Jones plummeted, the whole nation was absorbed with thoughts of one little girl. We learned again that small things and the life of an individual are what really matters as we watched the monumental rescue efforts focused on eighteen-month-old Jessica McClure, who had dropped twenty-two feet through an eight-inch opening in an oil pipeline. Drilling experts, highway construction equipment, pneumatic drills, special air vents, high-pressure hydraulic drills, and herculean effort were expended during the fifty-eight hours she was trapped underground. Rescuers tried everything possible in their mission to save the little girl.

Jesus came to make that same kind of effort to seek and to save that which is lost.

Many of Jesus' representatives could learn a lesson from His efforts to bring people back to God. When you look at evangelical religion today you see a great deal of narcissism, but not much interest in the lost. There is a defection of the baby-boomer generation from any organized religion. Those born from 1946 to 1962 do not demonstrate that much interest, even though some are coming back to church. Sociologists Wade Roof and William McKinney attribute this mass defection to the baby boomers' self-indulgent ethos that recognizes no bonds apart from personal choice, and regards society as a crowd of individuals strolling through a lifelong shopping mall of private purposes.

There is something woeful about anything that is lost—and something joyful about the one who is found. Just before Christmas 1986, six masterpieces by Edouard Vuillard were torn from their frames in a Paris museum, where they had hung since 1913. The paintings, worth three million dollars, were found the following February, prompting great joy throughout the art world.

Ephesians 2:10 says, "We are God's workmanship." The very word "workmanship" suggests a finished masterpiece, a work of art. God intends your life to be a masterpiece of His work. If you are a lost masterpiece, He's looking for you.

Now the tax collectors and "sinners" were all gathering around to hear him. But the Pharisees and the teachers of the law muttered, "This man welcomes sinners and eats with them."

Jesus continued: "There was a man who had two sons. The younger one said to his father, 'Father, give me my share of the estate.' So he divided his property between them.

"Not long after that, the younger son got together all he had, set off for a distant country and there squandered his wealth in wild living. After he had spent everything, there was a severe famine in that whole country, and he began to be in need. So he went and hired himself out to a citizen of that country, who sent him to his fields to feed pigs. He longed to fill his stomach with the pods that the pigs were eating, but no one gave him anything.

"When he came to his senses, he said, 'How many of my father's hired men have food to spare, and here I am starving to death! I will set out and go back to my father and say to him: 'Father I have sinned against heaven and against you. I am no longer worthy to be called your son; make me like one of your hired men.' So he got up and went to his father."

Luke 15:1–2, 11–19

2

Leaving Home

I wonder if there were a bulletin board in the Galilean Village in Jesus' story. I wonder if the anguished father, distraught but still hoping, might have tacked a notice there: "MISSING SON. Dark hair, dark eyes. Last seen carrying all his possessions down the road toward Diaspora."

It may be the greatest short story ever told, this parable of the lost son. It is the story of somebody, and everybody—the story of us all. And the Storyteller was Jesus.

The fifteenth chapter of Luke records a set of three parables included in no other Gospel. In the next chapter, we will see how the first two parables show how much Jesus wants to find those who have gone away from God. But in the parable of the lost son, the emphasis is on leaving—and being welcomed home.

We must remember that there was a very specific situation which caused Luke to save these three stories. The ministry of Jesus recorded in the Gospels is not at all like the modern church. Jesus was positively fascinating to the irreligious and antireligious sinners. All of the outcasts and runaways from God habitually and continually drew near to Him. This congregation of failures was not occasional—it gathered

13

again and again, wherever Jesus spoke. The most undesirable people constantly gathered to drink in His words.

By welcoming these followers, Jesus put the religious world of that day out of joint. He was the great disturber of the peace. Discussing Him, the religious leaders muttered back and forth to one another, not even using His name as they hissed like snakes, "Thissss man welcomes ssssinners and eats with them." Indeed, Jesus didn't just tolerate these sinners; he had a positive joy and pleasure in their company. In contrast, the religiously devout could not even approach wicked people on the street, no less eat with them.

Jesus responded to the Pharisees' mutterings by telling three stories. The greatest of these three is the dramatic parable about a boy who ran away, and then came back. And it is about the boy's father, who joyously welcomed him home. The story tells us that Jesus is acting like the father. Spiritually, many of us leave home; but He welcomes us back as an act of sheer grace.

GETTING AWAY FROM THE FATHER

The first part of this parable gives us insight about why we leave home spiritually. Any of us could make the decision that the essence, the real meaning, of human life is to get away from the heavenly Father. In this parable, the younger of two sons demands from his father his share of the estate. That is, he understood that the essence of life is the immediacy of fulfillment: "I want it all *now*." This boy was probably about seventeen and unmarried, because Jewish men in his day usually married at eighteen to twenty years of age.

In Jesus' world, a father could divide his estate before his death. The younger son would have received about two-ninths of the inheritance. But here was the hitch: If the father were alive, the son could possess his part of the inheritance, but he could not dispose of it or liquidate it until the father died. In this story, though, the boy wanted to have it all *and* dispose of

14

it. He wanted to treat his father as though he were already dead—nonexistent. He did not care that this would deprive him of all other claim on his father. He wanted it now, and he wanted it all—every last penny of it.

He wanted life in its totality and its immediacy. He was like Eve in the garden; she had every tree except one—but she wanted that one right now. All of us have been that way— whatever stuff there is in life, we want it all, and we want it now. We only go around once in life, and we grab the gusto. To many of us, "the gusto" is getting everything we can from the Father and getting away from Him—now.

Despite his son's treating him as if he were dead, the father in Jesus' parable gave the boy what he wanted. God is like that with all of the stuff of our lives, too. He showers it upon us—health, home, family, money, employment, friends, sunshine, air to breathe—all of it—even though we may stand at the door, ready to leave. As the psalmist said, "The Lord is good to all" (145:9), and as Peter said, "God is no respecter of persons" (Acts 10:34, KJV). Jesus summed it up this way: "He causes his sun to rise on the evil and the good" (Matt. 5:45).

In Jesus' story, the father gave the boy his share of the inheritance, with no strings attached—except the father's love for him. When his son demanded the stuff of life, the father simply handed it over. Compare that with the strange strings that have been attached to some modern wills. A Californian left sums to his granddaughters—provided they give up bobbed hair, rouge and powder, jewelry, dances, and movies, and that they wear dresses, "long at both ends." An exceedingly wealthy Englishman left his nephews a large sum—with the provision that they rise at five each morning and exercise for three hours. In 1953 a man left the Metropolitan Opera $150,000—with the stipulation they put on an awful opera he had written. The Met declined the offer.

The essence of getting away from the father is an urgency of independence. Luke 15:13 says, "Not long after that. . . ." the boy left. The inheritance was burning a hole in his pocket. There may have been a few days of respectful lingering; but his mind was already in another far country. When we have decided to get away from the Father there is a kind of hellish haste or ruinous rush. There has already been an inward separation; now that becomes an outward separation. When we decide that life is away from the Father, there is of necessity a haste, a running, a frenzy. Perhaps we have to run so fast to forget that, in truth, there *is* no life away from the Father.

This leads naturally to the desirability of distance: The son "set off for a distant country. . . ." This was not unusual in the world of Jesus, for emigration was the order of the day. Half a million Jews lived in Israel, but four million lived elsewhere throughout the known western world. Palestine often experienced famine, so it could even be prudent at times to emigrate. Apparently, though, there was more in this boy's belly than a fire for emigrating. He wanted all the stuff of life his father could give him; but more than anything else, he wanted to get away from his father.

To get away from the Father's care, restraint, protection, and boundary is the beginning of insanity in our lives today. When he left, the boy in the parable estranged and alienated himself from his past and his real life. Later in the parable, Jesus devotes only six words to his sin, saying the boy "squandered his wealth in wild living." There are no lurid details about how many women he slept with, what kind of parties he attended, how much alcohol he consumed. For Jesus, the essence of sin is not all of that voyeuristic detail. Instead, the essence of sin is when we think that the essence of life is to get away from the Father.

Jesus came to tell us that *life* is with the Father; *death* is away from the Father. You may think that the worst thing you can do spiritually is some specific, heinous sin. That is really not the case in the beginning. Spiritual suicide consists in this—in wanting to get away from the Father. Everything else simply follows from that.

THE REALITY OF LIFE AWAY FROM THE FATHER

Life away from the Father does not begin with dullness. It begins with a frenzy of activity. This boy wanted to travel first class—on the *Titanic*. And he did. What he had collected, he just as quickly scattered. The phrase "wild living" in verse 13 translates an expression which literally means "not to save." The boy was reckless, extravagant, and did not save anything for tomorrow. His life was a whirlwind of excitement, vitality, energy, and movement, with appointments to keep, people to see, deals to do—in an endless, dizzy excitement.

Life away from the Father always begins with busy vitality. You have to do that to mask the fact that it is just that—life away from the Father. I would emphasize again that Jesus did not give details of the boy's sin. Perhaps we would like that—a description of his activities. But Jesus would not lend any reality to what is ultimately unreal. Actual sin is like a black hole in outer space, like the Bermuda Triangle—it is unreal in the extreme. Only life with the Father is real.

While life away from the Father begins as a frenzy of activity, it continues with the loss of all resources. William Tronzo of Beaver Falls, Pennsylvania was earning seven thousand dollars a year in 1974. At forty-nine, he could barely buy clothes for his five children; they all shared one room in a rent house. Then he won a million dollars. He quit his job and began spending money. He bought diamonds for his wife, a new Thunderbird, six TV sets, insurance policies, and the house that had belonged to the lieutenant governor; he gave money to all his relatives—and in a few days discovered he was already thirty thousand dollars in debt. This led to extreme psychological problems.

Contemporary life contains many such striking examples of running through it all. Life away from the Father burns up resources. Time, emotional energy, willpower—they all burn out when we run away from the Father. Suddenly there are no resources left within us. There is, in effect, a "severe famine" throughout our lives. We begin to feel need, want, despair, anxiety, and loss of meaning. We learn the awful truth of life away from the Father. Jeremiah 2:13 states it clearly: "They have forsaken me the fountain of living waters, and hewed them out . . . broken cisterns . . ." (KJV). There is no more desolate feeling than to put all your chips on the table and say, "This is life" only to find out that the chips have vanished and the table was never even there.

Life away from the Father ends with degrading despair. Here is the irony. The boy's desire had been immediate, total independence. Instead, when the money runs out, he has to "glue" himself to a citizen of the distant country—attaching himself like a barnacle to a man who does not even want him. In that faroff country he has not gained a single friend. Away from your family, you do not find real pity, friendship, or sympathy. Since this man did not want the boy anyway, he sent him to do the worst imaginable job—to feed the swine. The Jews so hated swine that they called them *dabhar acher*, the other thing. Feeding them was an unclean occupation. For the Jew this meant the forfeiting of his religion—there could be no Sabbath, no kosher food. It was the worst thing imaginable.

Or was it? He would have been only too glad to have stuffed his belly with the carob pods he was feeding the pigs. These were long, coarse, sweetish bean-shaped pods the people used for fodder. He had the repeated, unfulfilled wish to gorge his empty stomach with the pig swill; but verse 16 says, "no one gave him anything."

Running away from the Father leaves us with the desire to fill the shouting, screaming emptiness of life with anything we can. It can be good things, such as housework, yardwork, churchwork, busywork. It can be bad things. But we want to fill the emptiness when we run away.

When we leave the Father, we experience total estrangement and alienation; we are uprooted, marooned, out of it, disconnected. Similarly, the boy in Jesus' story was estranged from his past, his future, his immediate environment, society, and from himself. Instead, here was a new self far different from the demanding, confident boy who left the father's house. The change in him was as great as that described by Pascal, who said, "There is no man more different from another than he is from himself at various times."

This is where life away from the Father, life that wants it all now, will leave you.

But Jesus told this story to hold out hope for those who have fallen this low. It is His promise that you are not too far away to come back. The hatefulness of our spiritual adversary is that the evil one puts us in this place—and then whispers, "It is too late to come back."

TURNING TOWARD HOME

Car developer John DeLorean rose to international fame, and then lost everything in a conviction for cocaine dealing to save his troubled company. He then professed conversion. Said DeLorean, "Foxhole conversions are legitimate. . . . Most of them in the Bible happened that way. When everything you ever wanted is happening, you are not inclined to reassess your priorities or to examine your spiritual values. When it all falls apart, it makes you take more than an ordinary look."

We start to come back to the Father when we understand the insanity of life apart from Him. This whole story turns on the words, "When he came to his senses. . . ." The words suggest awakening from a trance or a spiritual coma. The Hebrew means to stop being insane. To be saved, to be converted means to become rational, right-minded.

To a large extent, comas are a mystery. There is no reliable way to predict their outcome. In 1978 a team of doctors came up with what is known as the Glasgow Coma Scale. Based on eye, verbal, and motor responses, they assign a number on the scale to a confused or unconscious patient. Forty percent of the people who remain in a coma more than twenty-four hours die within two weeks. It is a rarity to be in a coma for weeks and then return to consciousness. But it does happen.

And even more mysterious than a physical coma is a spiritual one. If you assigned him a number on a spiritual coma scale, the lost son would have been close to the highest score. It is an act of sheer grace when a person awakens from such a state.

We start home when we deliberately move from lethargy and despair, when we say, as the boy did, "I will arise and go to my father" (KJV). This is somehow God's doing. But how He does it is a mystery. A spark suddenly flashes; a tiny flame blazes. A pulse suddenly beats and there is the stirring of life. The restoration of spiritual sanity came when the boy remembered that the very poorest people in his father's household had a better quality of life than he had. The hired men had an abundance of bread—while the boy had a scarcity of pig food. While he had been crying out, "Isn't this living?" he had really been living in misery. Remembering the grace of his father enlightened him.

This was the critical moment. When he came to his senses, he made himself move. He recognized the critical nature of the present moment in returning to his father. The past was gone, the future receding. This was the moment to get up.

On March 11, 1984, in the Westman Islands off of Iceland the seventy-four-foot trawler *Hellisey* overturned in a storm and Gudlaugur Fridthorsson made history. After falling into the 41-degree water, he should have soon died of hypothermia. When the body temperature goes below 93.2 degrees, blood flow to the brain is reduced. His two companions from the boat sank in twenty minutes. But Gudlaugur swam for six hours: breaststroke, backstroke, breaststroke, backstroke. As he was close to the shore a voice said to him, *Lie down and rest; you deserve it*. But a stern voice of reason argued, *If you go to*

20

sleep now, my lad, you will never wake up. Somehow Gudlaugur defied all laws of physiology and survived.

Sometimes coming back to God is just as dramatic as waking from a coma, as decisive as listening to the voice that calls to us in moments of crisis. Those times are the spiritual moments in our lives when we must tell ourselves, *If I go to sleep now, I will never wake up.* You can wake up; you can come back. But you must come back with urgency. Don't stop. Keep coming back.

For the director of music. Of David. A psalm.

I waited patiently for the Lord;
   he turned to me and heard my cry.
He lifted me out of the slimy pit,
   out of the mud and mire;
he set my feet on a rock
   and gave me a firm place to stand.
He put a new song in my mouth,
   a hymn of praise to our God.
Many will see and fear
   and put their trust in the Lord.

Blessed is the man
   who makes the Lord his trust,
who does not look to the proud,
   to those who turn aside to false gods.
Many, O Lord, my God,
   are the wonders you have done.
The things you planned for us
   no one can recount to you;
were I to speak and tell of them,
   they would be too many to declare.

Sacrifice and offering you did not desire,
   but my ears you have pierced;
burnt offerings and sin offerings
   you did not require.
Then I said, "Here I am, I have come—
   it is written about me in the scroll.
I desire to do your will, O my God;
   your law is within my heart."

Psalm 40:1–8

3

Out of Your Impossible Situation

Tony Chain, thirty-seven, and J. R. Hounchell, thirty-nine, went hunting the first day of duck season, September 1, 1981. They were in an area called Duck Flats northeast of Anchorage. Hours before, ten feet of tidal water had covered the gully where they now beached their boat. As they began their trudge through thick mud, Tony's left wader stuck fast. He yanked sharply against the ooze—but suddenly both feet were stuck. He tried to pitch forward, sideways. With each effort he sank deeper into the thick, gray glop.

Tony's chilling cry startled his hunting companion: "Quicksand! Help me, J. R.!" The two men had been hunting together for fifteen years. They both knew about Alaska's loose glacial silt—like quicksand. Formed by grains as small as talcum powder, the sand looks like common mud—but is far deadlier.

Gingerly stepping toward his friend, holding out the belt from his trousers, J. R. tried to help. Then he felt the surface become spongy beneath him. If he got caught, both of them would drown. He ran for help, knowing that time was against

23

them. Alaskan tides are among the fastest rising and most dangerous in the world. In less than four hours, the water would sweep across the flats, rising at a rate of one foot every twelve minutes.

J. R. was able to get through to Elmendorf Air Force Base, where a special rescue team scrambled to the site of the sinking man. But when the two Air Force rescuers tried to help Tony, they began to sink, too. One rescuer sank up to his thighs and the other rescuer had to rescue him. Everything they did seemed to worsen the situation.

Next, they passed a paddle seat attached to a helicopter and slipped the strap beneath Tony's arms. As the helicopter tried to hoist him up, Tony signaled frantically, his eyes wide with pain. The helicopter pilot knew that a similar rescue attempt some time ago had torn the victim in two at the waist.

The only possibility was to decrease the distance between Tony and the chopper, so that he could be pulled more slowly from the mud. That meant hovering directly overhead. The pilot lowered the helicopter to thirty, twenty, then ten feet, seven . . . six feet above the muck. Tony yelled, "No lower, no lower!" At this point a gust of wind could have blown the copter down and broken his back.

By 1:45 P.M. the mud was up to Tony's armpits. The tide could come in at almost any time. Suddenly, there was a slight movement upward. Little by little, Tony felt the waders slip off his legs and disappear into the bog as he was pulled free at last—just in the nick of time. (*Reader's Digest*, August 1986, pp. 115F.)

GOD RESCUES US FROM IMPOSSIBLE SITUATIONS

Like Tony Chain, the psalmist found himself in great difficulty. But unlike Tony, the psalmist's troubles seemed to be beyond even the greatest human effort. His own efforts only proved the final futility of the problem. But God intervened, and the psalmist responded to that intervention with a fresh sense of praise and a new demonstration of obedience.

By asking God alone to act, you can find a way out of your difficult situation. No matter how impossible things seem, you can come back to God.

The psalmist's words present a memorable picture of human helplessness: "He lifted me out of the slimy pit, out of the mud and mire." The words picture a deep pit where even deeper waters resound from a horrible cavern further below. Such pits were used as dungeons (Jer. 38:6), pitfalls for wild beasts (Ps. 7:15), or even as a grave (Ps. 28:1). The words could also refer to a horrible pit of desolation, a roaring, resounding pit of spiritual tumult. The noise could be that of water at the bottom of the pit. Or the noise could refer to the screams of soldiers, their armor crashing and clanging as they plunged into its depths.

We can imagine that the bottom of the pit was a muck of filthy mire. The more the psalmist struggled to get out, the deeper he sank into the bog. Such places were found at the bottom of disused cisterns in the Holy Land. Jeremiah had known the experience of being placed in just such a place as this while he was a prisoner of conscience for his preaching. The depth, the noise, and the sinking slime all add up to an unforgettable picture of an impossible situation.

What kind of experience led the psalmist to express himself this way? It may have been a military defeat, the opposition of wicked people, sickness, or the impossible situation created by personal sin in his life. We do not know—and perhaps that is best. Not knowing the cause, we can identify our own impossible situation with the psalmist's.

Where is your place of absolute impossibility? Is it a relationship? You never meant it to become what it has become, but now there is nothing you can do about it. Is it a habit? At first it seemed harmless, superficial, nonthreatening. You thought you could stop at any time you desired. But now, like

Tony in the quicksand, you are trapped. Is it a bitterness, a gnawing thing within you that sours all of life and makes every day heavy with the desire for revenge? Is it a past failure, a sin, a lapse you thought was impossible for you? Now the horizon of every day hangs heavy with the sense that you have crushed something that can never be repaired, broken something that can never be mended. Is it a loss, a loss so profound that life has lost all significance and you really have no desire to go on?

Suddenly God moves into the difficulty and the entire situation changes. From the bottom of a pit, the psalmist is elevated to the safety of a rocky cliff. Sinking in the instability of the bog, he suddenly finds sure footing on stable ground. God not only gave him present safety but also future stability. Immersed in a threat that would have ended life, the future opened before him. It all happened so suddenly—because of the intervention of God.

Another example, this time from the animal world, shows how God makes provision for stability in the most difficult circumstances. In bold defiance of gravity, the mountain goats that live from the Northwest United States through Canada into Alaska demonstrate incredible stability in the most difficult of terrains. They leap surefootedly from mountain ledge to mountain ledge, scampering around steep, rugged mountainsides with the utmost confidence. Unusually flexible, the two toes of the goat's hoof can spread apart wider than the hoof is long to distribute the animal's grip. Or they can draw together to grasp a knob of rock. The goat also has a rough, pliable traction pad on the bottom of each toe which makes them skid-resistant on ice. Dewclaws projecting from the rear of the ankles provide additional traction on steep, downhill routes.

Just as God makes provision in the animal world for creatures to stand with stability in the most difficult of terrain, He will surely make provision for His redeemed children to stand in the most difficult spiritual circumstances. He can and will stabilize you in the midst of insuperable difficulty.

The Bible includes many stories describing how God dealt with impossible situations. We believe these stories. We believe that God gave Abraham a baby when the old man was ninety-nine and his wife Sarah was almost as old. We believe that God used an eighty-year-old, tongue-tied shepherd to pull off the Exodus. We believe that God marched a ragtag army of Hebrew slaves around Jericho and the walls came tumbling down. We believe a teen-age boy killed a giant with a stone, and a handful of fishermen turned the world upside down with the message of Christ. We believe that the God of the Bible could do all this.

And what is more, we believe that God can do this today for others, even for our friends. If a friend came to you with the confession of some great failure, you would pray for him or her, and offer the reminder that God can rescue His people from anything.

We believe all this—as long as it is in the Bible or happening to somebody else. But Psalm 40 means that God can deal with the impossibility of *your* life!

How do you make this happen? The secret is in verse 1: "I waited patiently for the Lord; he turned to me and heard my cry." There is an emphatic repetition in the original language: "I waited, yea, I waited." The resounding of the words indicates a total reliance on God alone to extricate him. This also suggests an exclusive waiting on God: "I simply waited; I did nothing but wait." You must deliberately and exclusively wait on the intervention of the Lord. The opposite of waiting on God is to fret, be angry, and to take things into your own hands (Ps. 37:7).

God may place you in an impossible situation where only a divine act can deliver you. But the promise is that God will hear and respond to those who ask for His help. The image is that of one leaning forward to catch a faint or distant sound. The God of the cosmos hears and intervenes for those who cry to Him.

We've heard stories of how waiting has saved people

from impossible situations here on earth. For example, there's the story of Barry Beck, a thirty-four-year-old geology professor and a veteran of caving, who led a group from the Georgia Southwestern College Outdoor Club on an expedition to Anderson Springs Cave in the Appalachians of northern Georgia. By 4:30 on Saturday afternoon they had been in the cave five hours, following an underground stream that was nearly a mile beneath Pigeon Mountain. Suddenly the stream began to rise. Where water had been dripping from the walls, it suddenly came gushing out like water from fire hoses. What they did not know was that the hardest rain to hit the mountain in fifty years had created tons of water pressure on top of the cave.

The spelunkers made their way back upstream to a large cavern and climbed to a ledge about forty feet above the rising water. Their teeth chattering, their limbs jerking, they knew of the possibility of hypothermia, shock, and coma. Finally, Beck found a sort of den under the cave roof. To keep warm, they stacked themselves in like cord wood. Then there was nothing they could do but wait in the pit and listen to the roar of the rushing water. Their situation seemed impossible—until a scuba diver made his way up the roaring underground river thirty hours after their ordeal began. They had to wait; they had no other choice. (*Reader's Digest*, July 1980, pp. 55–58)

Similarly, God sometimes makes us wait for His intervention. Psalm 46 records a situation where God's people needed His help, but He did not intervene until the last moment: "God will help her at the break of day" (verse 5). After waiting throughout the night for divine help, the people were about to give up. At the peep of dawn, the last possible moment before their enemy invaded, God demonstrated His power to rescue.

Sometimes God waits until we and everyone around us clearly see that our only hope is His intervention. God also waits because there is a renewal of our strength in the process of waiting. "But those who hope in the Lord will renew their strength. They will soar on wings like eagles; they will run and not grow weary, they will walk and not be faint" (Isa. 40:31). Literally, those who wait on God "exchange" their weakness for strength. When we are spent, tired, and exhausted we need to exchange our spentness for His power. We feel like a flat tire. We wait on God. He fills us with Himself again. In the act of waiting, there is an exchange of our emptiness for His fullness.

RESPONDING APPROPRIATELY TO GOD'S DELIVERY

How do we respond when God rescues us from an impossible situation? We can respond first with fresh praise to God: "He put a new song in my mouth." How long has it been since you have praised God with a new song?

God had done such a dramatic new thing in the psalmist's life that none of the old psalms would do. He wrote a new victory hymn celebrating God's recent deliverance in his life. The emphasis rests on the new quality of the song, not just its recent composition. The phrase may suggest constantly new songs, each one succeeding the other as daily new material offers itself for praise. Or the word may suggest newness in the sense of being always fresh and full of life. The believer lives constantly with that sense of newness: a new name (Rev. 2:17), new commandment (John 13:34), new covenant (Heb. 8:8), new Jerusalem (Rev. 21:2), new man (Eph. 2:15).

God can bring fresh praise out of both tragedy and glory, as illustrated by this story about a favorite hymn. Luther Bridgers began preaching at age seventeen while he was a student at Asbury College in Kentucky. He was a young Methodist minister of unusual zeal and evangelism. In 1910 the future looked bright for the twenty-six-year-old preacher, who by then had a young wife and three children. The Bridgers family was visiting Mrs. Bridgers's parents at Harrodsburg, Kentucky. After the family retired for the night, a neighbor noticed flames coming from the house. He roused Mrs. Bridgers's parents and

Luther, but the rest of the family members were beyond reach. The young pastor lost his wife and children.

In the awful days of sorrow that followed, Luther remembered that God offered songs of comfort in the night (Ps. 42:8), and would never forsake him. It was during this period that Luther wrote the words and music that we sing so many times: "There's within my heart a melody / Jesus whispers sweet and low / fear not, I am with thee, peace be still; in all of life's ebb and flow." In the fourth stanza he referred to his own experience: "Tho sometimes he leads through waters deep / trials fall across the way. . . ."

In the darkest night, in the depths of despair, God gave an inward song to Luther Bridgers that blesses millions. Out of a pit of grief came a song of blessing.

Part of the reason for the psalmist's new song was the impact of God's intervention on those who observed his life: "Many will see and fear and put their trust in the Lord" (Ps. 40:3). God's act will compel the attention of bystanders to the power of God. Does anything in your life do that?

You can also respond with a new obedience when God rescues you from impossible situations. When the psalmist struggled with how to express gratitude toward such a delivering God, he weighed all of the outward religious rituals of his day. Animal sacrifices, meal offerings of fine flour, burnt offerings indicating total dedication, and sin offerings propitiating God all presented themselves as possible ways to indicate gratitude. But God does not want ritual; He wants reality. He desires us to be in harmony with Him rather than perform ceremonies for Him.

The psalmist expresses that he has heard God: "my ears you have pierced." This unusual phrase meant that God had broken through at a new level of speaking to the inward person. The result of that is an immediate sense of obedience to the will of God: "Then I said, 'Here I am, I have come.'" These are the characteristic words of a servant who comes immediately to do the will of the master.

When will we learn that God wants obedience and reality above all else? Everything else is ritual. The only real response to God's intervention in your life is to hear and obey. When you do so, you will have a fresh song for God to sing tomorrow and every day.

When you come back to God, He meets you at your point of impossibility.

This is what the Lord says:

"Cursed is the one who trusts in man,
    who depends on flesh for his strength
    and whose heart turns away from the Lord.
He will be like a bush in the wastelands;
    he will not see prosperity when it comes.
He will dwell in the parched places of the desert,
    in a salt land where no one lives.

"But blessed is the man who trusts in the Lord,
    whose confidence is in him.
He will be like a tree planted by the water
    that sends out its roots by the stream.
It does not fear when heat comes;
    its leaves are always green.
It has no worries in a year of drought
    and never fails to bear fruit."

The heart is deceitful above all things
    and beyond cure.
    Who can understand it?

"I the Lord search the heart
    and examine the mind,
to reward a man according to his conduct,
    according to what his deeds deserve."

Jeremiah 17:5–10

4

Whom Do You Trust?

The question, "Whom do you trust?" may be silly or serious. For some, the question reminds us of a superficial television game show named "Who Do You Trust?" that was hosted by Johnny Carson from 1957 to 1962. In the show, two married couples were interviewed. When asked a question, the husband had the opportunity to answer the question for himself or to trust his wife with the answer to the question. After five years of pressure from English grammarians, the name of the show was changed to "Whom Do You Trust?" and Carson departed for the "Tonight Show."

In contrast to the trivial nature of the game-show question, "Whom do you trust?" is neither silly nor superficial when it relates to life's ultimate source of reliance. We all have to face the ultimate question of human existence—where do I deposit my final, total trust? There are two options. You deposit your confidence in God and God alone—or somewhere else. When you lodge your trust in God, you flourish. When you place your faith in anything else, you fade—you turn away from God.

Total trust cannot be divided. It is indivisible, all or nothing. When you trust one thing you cannot trust another. Trust

33

in God alone is not compatible with trust in your own cleverness. When you trust your own resources, you turn away from God.

This scripture reveals an inner battle in Jeremiah's life. He conducted a debate with himself about where his trust should land. Then Jeremiah faced hardship, rejection, mockery, and contempt because he preached trust in an invisible Jehovah God rather than the very visible, material powers of his own generation. Jeremiah's contemporaries could readily see the power, wealth, and armies of Egypt and Assyria. They could not see Jehovah, God of their ancestors. Jeremiah's people wanted to trust the big battalions, to go with the winners, and ultimately, even Jeremiah himself was shaken to the very center of his own belief. *Will I trust God or will I trust what everyone else trusts in my generation?* he worried to himself.

Jeremiah chose God. Was he right? Consider this: Everything else from Jeremiah's world is gone today; but the book of the prophet Jeremiah stands as a monument to trust in God and God alone.

Where have you placed your trust? Have you turned away from God? As you begin the decade of the nineties, your well-being depends on your total trust in God and God alone—not in yourself, your family, your vocation, or your network.

THE RELIANCE THAT CURSES LIFE

Life without total trust in God is life lived under a self-imposed curse. Our text opens, "This is what the Lord says." The Eternal One gives you a revelation about your life, a revelation you could not discover unless He revealed it to you. It is simply this: Life that places its ultimate reliance on mere humans curses itself. God does not desire to put life under a hex. He sent His Son that you might have life. But when you put your ultimate confidence in man rather than God, you yourself put your life under an inherent curse. It is as certain as the law of gravity that makes you fall when you lean too far.

34

The reason for a life that curses itself is misplaced trust: "Cursed is the one who trusts in man" (v.5). When a person puts ultimate confidence in other persons, that person leans the weight of his or her whole life on a pile of dust. The Hebrew language is graphic, material, and energetic. The Hebrew word for trust (*batah*) means "to throw oneself forward toward an object in order to rest on the object." The word "man" reflects someone who is made from dust and who returns to dust. Genesis 3:19 tells the truth: "dust you are and to dust you will return."

This reminds me of the story about a little boy who asked his mother this question after church one Sunday: "Is it true that God made us from dust?" His mother answered, "Yes, the Bible says He did." To her surprise, the lad led her to his room and lifted his bedspread. 'If people are made of dust," he said, "I thought you ought to know that someone is either coming or going under my bed." When you place ultimate trust in anything merely human, you lean the weight of your entire existence on nothing more than dust.

To put it another way, Jeremiah points out the curse on life that comes from leaning on a merely human arm for life's support rather than on the arm of God. Again, the Hebrews thought of God in a very literal, physical, tangible language. To trust God was to lean on His strong, faithful arm. When God Himself had rescued the Hebrews from their abject slavery in Egypt, He told them in Exodus 6:6, "I will redeem you with an outstretched arm." God's people were to lean on God's invisible but very real arm of strength. Instead, they leaned on the arm of flesh. They leaned on themselves and other mere human arms—arms that perished, weakened, and decayed. Over and over the prophets warned against trusting the strength of a human arm rather than the divine arm of Jehovah God.

Since 1887, Christians have sung the stirring gospel song "What a fellowship, what a joy divine / Leaning on the everlasting arms. . . . / Leaning, leaning / Leaning on the everlasting arms." Those words were written by A. J. Showalter after he received letters from two friends, both of whom had lost their wives. He wrote to them the scripture, "The eternal God is your refuge, and underneath are the everlasting arms" (Deut. 33:27). As he pondered these words, the favorite hymn came to Showalter and he penned the words to our song.

You *will* lean on something—but what? You can reveal what that something is if you give your honest first impression to the following statement: "If everything fell apart I would. . . ." Would you trust your appearance, fitness, intelligence, or health? Would you trust your family? Would you trust your vocation? Would you trust your personal network of friends? If the heat were really on, how would you answer?

Despair is the result of living life away from God, under the curse of self-trust. When you fail to trust God alone, you are diminished, deprived, and deserted. To demonstrate the despair of a life that refuses to trust God, Jeremiah uses poetic language. He tells us what such a person is like—"a bush in the wastelands." He tells us what this person misses—everything that counts. He tells us where this person lives—in a spiritual wilderness.

Refusal to put your total trust in God leads to a diminished life away from His presence—a life like that of "a bush in the wastelands." The word means a barren, dry, stunted growth of scrub brush. It refers to the juniper tree, which inhabits the most barren and rocky parts of the desert, as well as lonely crags and inaccessible fissures on rocky cliffs. It was inaccessible except to the goats—which stripped it naked of all its leaves.

What is life like when you refuse to trust God? It's like a dried, dwarfed, desolate bush stripped of even the few leaves that it had! A person who puts ultimate trust in anyone other than God barely ekes out existence—while God offers life in abundance.

Refusal to trust God alone not only diminishes life and leads to despair. It also deprives life. "He will not see prosperity when it comes." The person who refuses to trust God is blind to the goodness He gives. This blindness is shown in a new disease suffered by many affluent people around the country. It is called "affluenza," a horde of paralyzing emotional and psychic fears that sometimes accompany affluence. "Affluenza" can strike lottery winners, newly minted professionals with great earning power, or those who merely inherit a fortune. An example is the young woman from an affluent family who lived in opulent homes in Manhattan, Bal Harbor, Florida, and on Lake Superior's Madeline Island, traveling between them in the family plane, helicopter, and a yellow Rolls Royce. At age twenty-one she received a two-million-dollar inheritance. Now, at thirty-six, she confesses long-held feelings of guilt, isolation, and impotence. Many are terrified of losing the fortunes they have, and so they exist in loneliness. If you do not put your ultimate confidence in God, you will not see the good when it is all around.

What about you? Do you see goodness and blessings all around? Or do you carp and complain because of the absence of things? That is a good index to your trust of God.

Refusal to trust God also means a deserted life away from Him. Such a person "will dwell in the parched places of the desert, in a salt land where no one lives." Life without trust in God is lived in spiritual burnt places, in emotional lava beds. Life without God is lived as if on salty soil, uninhabited and uninhabitable.

At the south end of the Dead Sea is a strange salt mountain six miles long and 650 feet high, as well as an impassable salty mud flat. Visitors are usually overwhelmed by a sense of desolation and destruction. Nothing lives in it or around it. This awful isolation rounds out Jeremiah's picture of the life that does not trust God.

The disgraced Ivan Boesky is the incarnation of Jeremiah's prophecy and the very symbol of life in the late 1980s. Born and reared in Detroit, he was the son of a Russian immigrant. From childhood, he was driven by the desire to excel, performing hundreds of pushups at a time. He married the daughter of a real estate tycoon, but his in-laws called him, "Ivan the Bum." Drifting through three colleges before earning a law degree, he arrived on Wall Street at age twenty-nine. Sleeping two or three hours a night, rising at 4:30 each morning, he stood behind a desk and punched buttons on a three-hundred-line telephone console. He craved coffee and information. But twenty-hour workdays, a ten-bedroom house on two hundred acres near New York, and a fortune of $200 million was not enough. No amount convinced him that he had finally arrived. Then he was convicted of trading stock with illegal inside information, and it all collapsed. He had to withdraw from prominent trusteeships, directorships, and charities. He was barred from securities dealing for life. Every desire of his life was lost. Somewhere Ivan trusted only Ivan. The result was a life that was diminished, deprived, and deserted.

You may think there's no comparison between the scale of Ivan Boesky's lifestyle and your own. But you can lose confidence in God on any size playing field. Your name may never be in a newspaper headline; but you may suffer the same desolation and isolation on another scale because you trusted man and not God. Ultimate reliance on mere humans curses life.

THE BLESSINGS OF ULTIMATE RELIANCE ON GOD

Life can and should be lived under the blessing of God. As Jeremiah wrote, "Blessed is the man who trusts in the Lord, whose confidence is in him." When you place your total confidence in God alone, there are resources available, responses achievable, and reactions demonstrable that give life the deepest sense of well-being.

Life that trusts God alone finds faithful resources: "He will be like a tree planted by the water." In Jeremiah 2:13, God calls Himself "the spring of living water." What a contrast! The man refusing to trust God is stunted in a wasteland. The man who trusts God is sending down roots into an ever-flowing source of life. Trust in God means an abundance of

38

available resources, regardless of the external situation. Further, such resources may be hidden from others, but nevertheless they are spiritually real and refreshing. Jesus stood at the great feast in Jerusalem to cry out a truth for you, "Whoever believes in me, as Scripture has said, streams of living water will flow from within him" (John 7:38). By living water, He meant the Spirit, a hidden source of renewed life inside the believer.

The resources of life God gives are not only available and hidden, they are abundant. "Streams of living water" means a plentiful supply. If one stream should fail, there are many other streams. There is always an abundance of resources for divine life. An earthly example of such a tree is the Bald Cyprus. It grows in the deep swamps and rivers of the Southeast, sometimes achieving diameters of thirteen feet. Some are as old as 950 years because they grow in a never-ending surplus of water that gives life. Similarly, God says, "Put your confidence in me and you will be like the cyprus that grows in a never-ending surplus of abundant water."

Best of all, this promise of the rewards of total trust speaks of a source that is independent of the immediate environment. A tree that can thrust its roots into a river survives in a drought because the stream still flows even though rain does not fall. Life that deposits all trust in God alone is promised such an endless resource. You may say, "I am not living there. I am like the juniper scrub brush." But the good news is that you can transplant your life. You don't have to live away from God. One scholar interprets the tree in Jeremiah 17:8 as being transplanted from desolation to abundance. If you refuse to trust man alone and deposit trust in God, your life is transplanted.

Life that trusts God alone makes a vital response, just like the tree that "sends out its roots by the stream." This tree is not inert. Jeremiah says literally, "It thrusts out its roots to the waterbrooks." There is vitality, energy, direction, growth. When I encounter the life of God, I will actively and energetically thrust myself deeper and deeper into the great Source of life. While life without God dwarfs, withers, and retreats, life in God grows and flourishes. A seed can be completely dry, its life suspended for years. It can withstand temperatures high and low. But when it comes into contact with water it will grow roots, and those roots will be covered with innumerable root hairs that will penetrate the most minute crannies of the soil to take in every bit of moisture. Life in God is like that. When we come to life, when the seed of life germinates within us, we thrust out our roots deeper and deeper into the divine life. The more we really trust, the more we want to trust.

As a result of all this, the life that trusts God alone demonstrates stable reactions. In times of adversity, "It does not fear when heat comes." Similarly, "It has no worries in a year of drought." A tree with hidden streams of water survives adversity of heat and insufficiency of water. A man or woman with total trust sunk deep into God's life likewise cannot only endure but thrive in adversity and insufficiency.

Do you have that kind of inner resource? When life is under attack, do you have a fortress with inner provisions that can withstand the siege? Between the two world wars, the French built an eighty-seven-mile-long defensive wall called the Maginot Line—the great wall of France that defended its border with Germany. Three lines of defense were incorporated into the wall. The first were strong houses, small fortified barracks designed to sound the alarm. The second line of defense was deep, reinforced bunkers to delay enemy attack. But the third line of defense was called *ouvrage*, deeply buried multi-storied forts every four to six miles. Below the barracks, at the deepest level, were the storehouses of ammunition, food, and above all else, a constant supply of water from deep wells.

When the Germans did move against France, they did not even try to attack these final forts. Not a single one of the *ouvrage* was ever overcome or taken by the Germans. Why? The Germans knew the soldiers in these bunkers could survive and resist almost indefinitely because of the deep, endless supply of water.

All of us need fortifications for life. But every line of defense is inadequate unless deep within us there is a resource hidden, abundant, untouchable. When the assault of life's enemy comes, we need not fear if that Source is within us. Absolute trust in God means that Source of life can never be taken. Come what may—rejection, poverty, loss of vocation, misunderstanding—Jeremiah himself experienced all of that and more. Yet what was true for him can be true for you. Jesus said it best: from within, streams of living water.

WHERE YOUR RELIANCE REALLY RESTS

How do I know whether my ultimate trust rests in God or in humans? Only God Himself can reveal that to me. I dare not trust my own unaided reflection.

You cannot know your own heart without His help. "The heart is deceitful above all things." This description of "the heart" means that whole complex of thoughts and emotions, conflicts, drives, and motives that make up the hidden, inner lives of people. The Word of God calls the heart crooked, twisted, and devious. This by no means says that everyone is a miscreant, a degenerate. It does mean that no one—not little children or old men—can read his own heart. The Hebrew word suggests that the heart follows our footsteps for the purpose of betraying us. The human heart is as intricate as a maze, as intriguing as a riddle. It is an inaccessible recess and a dark cavern. This does not just refer to other people's hearts as I relate to them, although that is true enough. No one can know fully his neighbor's thoughts or motives. But these words mean more than that. I cannot know my own heart without God's help.

Our hearts can present to us an illusion, a mirage. We admit the reality and the presence of illusions in the natural world. On U.S. 90 between Alpine and Marfa, Texas, people stop to look for the Marfa lights. In the distant flats of that remote Big Bend area, people have reported strange lights for years. A disk of light will move across a field, zigzag, and divide. Some think it is methane gas; others cite phosphorescent minerals, and still others say the lights are the reflections of car lights or starlight in the dust of the flatlands. After a hundred years of guessing, no one can say what the illusion really is. But it is definitely there.

The Wild West of yesteryear was full of illusions on distant horizons. One of George Custer's young officers was sure he saw a party of Indians at a mile's distance. As the soldiers charged, the Indians looked plainer each moment. But arriving at the point, there were no Indians at all—only some buffalo carcasses. Other travelers saw ships skimming across the desert sand in full sail, railroad tracks elevated on pilings, or water birds with brilliant plumage. All of these illusions occur when light rays pass through the atmosphere, bent and distorted.

But no optical illusions in nature exceed the illusions that can be left by our own hearts. By diagnosis, the human spiritual heart is "beyond cure." Unaided by God, the response of each of us toward knowing his or her heart must be despair: "Who can know it?" No one can fathom the secrets or pierce the darkness of his or her own heart. This is especially true at the point of the question about whom we trust—here again, our hearts can fool.

But there is hope. It rests in this: God knows your heart (v. 10). He sifts, searches, explores, and probes the human heart. He tests and examines human emotions. This is our hope. When we get to know God, we get to know our own heart. You do not know your heart by looking into it, yourself. You know your heart by getting to know God through our Lord Jesus Christ.

In the natural world, science can penetrate what before could never be seen. Geologists at Harvard and MIT use a special scanning device to penetrate to the very core of the earth, the very heart of our planet. But there is no one to scan the depths of the human heart except God Himself.

The Son of God, the Lord Jesus Christ, knows your heart. John 2:25 tells us, "He did not need man's testimony about man, for he knew what was in a man." He repeatedly X-rayed the deepest motives of His friends, family, followers, and foes. The risen Jesus Christ quoted the very words of this Old Testament text, proclaiming, when He spoke to the ancient church in Thyatira, "Then all the churches will know that I am he who searches hearts and minds" (Rev. 2:23).

Do you really want to know your own heart? Then come back to God. Place your total confidence, your ultimate trust in the Lord Jesus Christ. He will reveal your heart to you. But far more than that, He will make you like a tree planted by streams of water. He will give you unfailing, faithful, abundant resources for all of life. Why not begin with total surrender and total trust toward Him?

For the director of music. According to gittith.
Of the Sons of Korah. A psalm.

How lovely is your dwelling place,
    O Lord Almighty!
My soul yearns, even faints,
    for the courts of the Lord;
my heart and my flesh cry out
    for the living God.

Even the sparrow has found a home,
    and the swallow a nest for herself,
    where she may have her young—
a place near your altar,
    O Lord Almighty, my King and my God.
Blessed are those who dwell in your house;
    they are ever praising you. Selah.

Blessed are those whose strength is in you,
    who have set their hearts on pilgrimage.
As they pass through the Valley of Baca,
    they make it a place of springs;
    the autumn rains also cover it with pools.
They go from strength to strength,
    till each appears before God in Zion.

Hear my prayer, O Lord God Almighty;
    listen to me, O God of Jacob. Selah
Look upon our shield, O God;
    look with favor on your anointed one.

Better is one day in your courts
    than a thousand elsewhere;
I would rather be a doorkeeper in the house of my God
    than dwell in the tents of the wicked.
For the Lord God is a sun and shield;
    the Lord bestows favor and honor;
no good thing does he withhold
    from those whose walk is blameless.

O Lord Almighty,
    blessed is the man who trusts in you.

Psalm 84

5

Longing for the Lord

One of the most popular modern pastimes is looking back. We live in a haze of nostalgia, longing for another time. As illogical as it may seem, many in their twenties and thirties feel a longing akin to homesickness for a time they never knew. Students of nostalgia tell us that people in the 1970s looked back with longing to the forties and fifties. In 1971 more than fifty thousand copies of *Buck Rogers* were reprinted and three hundred radio stations brought back the serials from the thirties and forties such as "The Shadow," and "The Green Hornet." The forties seemed faraway and romantic to people growing up in the seventies. Now there is a nostalgia for the fifties and sixties, shown in the current popularity of hair cuts, slang, and the music of that earlier time.

Similarly, in Psalm 84 the psalmist showed a longing for an earlier time. This was no shallow escape, however. With something akin to homesickness, he longed to return to the place where he used to meet with God. He wanted to get back to the time and place where he could know God again. He acknowledged that such a return is a pilgrimage, a journey that has obstacles and difficulties. Yet he longed to get back to the place where he could meet the living God.

When you desire to return to the place where you meet God, faith overcomes every obstacle until you arrive. Are you homesick for God? Here's a map to find the way back.

LONGING FOR THAT PLACE

Once there was a place, a setting, a situation, a location where God was real to you. God was not real *because* of that place, but the place is significant because God was there. For Abraham it was Bethel. For Moses it was Mt. Sinai. For Jesus it was Gethsemane.

In this psalm the writer longs for the place where he used to meet with God. Now he is a prisoner, or in exile, or is ill, or for some other reason cannot get back to the place where he used to meet with God—the temple in Jerusalem. Can you identify with the man who is away from the place where he used to meet with God?

He expresses this in the language of a love poem: "How lovely is your dwelling place." The temple, the place where God was dwelling, was worthy to be loved. It is difficult to understand the impression that the temple of Solomon made on the Hebrew worshiper. David proposed the temple and amassed the materials. A hundred thousand talents of gold and a million talents of silver were collected from the people. When he had donated gold from his own fortune and that of the other princes, the building contained something like the equivalent of $4.9 billion in precious metals. It took seven years and six months to complete. Thirty thousand Israelites and 150,000 Canaanites were impressed as hewers of stone, carriers of water, and builders of the building. God's presence in the temple was overwhelming in the dimensions of the place. In the Old Testament world you met the living God in the massive, gold-covered cedar beams and the stonework of that building.

We no longer yearn for a physical temple, a building, an edifice in the same way as the Old Testament person did. Today, the gathering of believers individually and collectively

46

is the temple of God (1 Cor. 3:16; 6:19). In the Old Testament, God had a temple for His people. In the New Testament, He has a people for His temple. What is the equivalent longing today for what the psalmist felt for the temple in Jerusalem? It is the longing to be with the people of God in the place where they assemble to meet the living God. The modern equivalent of Psalm 84:1 is to long for an experience with the living God in the very midst of others who long for that same experience.

Longing for God creates an intensity of spirit. A modern-day example of intensity might be illustrated by the amateur athletes who compete every four years in the Olympic games. We wonder how people find the drive to achieve such records. One such athlete is Andy Sudduth, who competes in rowing—pulling the oars in a single scull, a slight crimson shell of a canoe. Even though he has injured his ribs, he rows on. Even though he has had to cut back his job as a computer analyst at Harvard University, he continues to press. He postponed working on a master's degree at Harvard in order to train. "You put your life on hold," he said. "It happens to everyone in rowing. . . ."

We often find such intensity in those who compete. But do we expect the same intensity in ourselves when we want to come back to God? Are we willing to "put everything on hold" until we find the place where we meet God again? The psalmist's words express this kind of passion. Listen to the language of a man who wants to get back to God. He "yearns, faints, cries out for the living God." The word "yearns" depicts someone who longs and pines to the extent of growing pale.

Would you characterize the intensity of your desire for God with those words? This man "faints" with longing for the exterior courts of the temple of God. The phrase suggests that his heart virtually fails, because he is so consumed just to stand in the outer court of the place where he meets with God.

Remember that this is a man who looked back to animal sacrifices and the smoke of the brazen altar. Yet this man yearns, faints, and cries out for the place where he meets God.

If he did so with such intensity, how much more intensity should we feel who look back to Calvary and to the opened, empty tomb—we who have found life and immortality through Jesus Christ? There is a totality within the intensity as the psalmist's soul, his heart, and his flesh all cry out for the living God. This is no partial devotion to God in which the emotions feel Him, but the mind does not think of Him, and the will does not bend to Him. This man is an electrified, animated, pulsating whole person, every part of whom intensely desires the encounter with God!

Longing for God also reflects an integrity of intention, as shown when the worshiper cries out for the living God. Psalm 84:2 is only one of two places in the Old Testament where God is called "the living God" (see also Psalm 42:1). That is, the psalmist desires to contact God Himself as He really is. He does not long for the house of God so much as for the God whose house it is. He wants to keep the primary thing the primary thing. When you go to a courthouse you do not seek the courtroom, but justice. At the hospital you are not going for the building itself, but because it is a place to get well. You do not attend a school because the school is an end in itself, but because that is the place you get an education.

Many secondary things can happen at the place where God's people meet. Someone may mumble in the pew before you, a fly may buzz past you, twinges of boredom may set in while the sermon drones on, pangs of regret may fill your mind about things you did not get done the past week. Or you may have better experiences and still not long for God. You may be overwhelmed by the architecture of the building, or be carried away by the beauty of the music. You may laugh at the pastor's joke, or be impressed by the size of the crowd. But none of that is an encounter with the living God. The difference between going to church and encountering the living God is the difference between reading a lecture on atomic energy and watching an atomic bomb explode.

The purpose of this entire institution ought to be to meet the living God. Why do churches buy property, pave parking lots, build buildings, employ large staffs, organize, administer programs, hold endless meetings, buy literature, train choirs, raise a budget, and a thousand other things? Never, never that these things would be an end in themselves. Churches become a travesty if all of these secondary things become primary. We must always weigh everything we do against the question, "How does this enable us to meet the living God?"

Longing for God reveals an intimacy of desire. Lovers envy anything that is near the loved one. The psalmist recalls that swallows and sparrows nest in the temple area close to the place where he once met God. Away, exiled, debarred from the presence of God, he envies anything that is closer to that place than he is.

In the ancient East, birds nesting in a temple were considered sacred. To this day, birds are allowed to nest in the Mosque of Omar near the Old Testament temple site. Temples have often been sanctuaries for birds. An hour's drive from Bangkok, Thailand is the Wat Phai Lom, an ancient Buddhist temple. In its enclosure is a riotous gathering of seventeen thousand openbill storks, the largest gathering of such birds in the world. It is a sanctuary for those birds.

The psalmist remembers a scene like that. He recalls that some of God's lower creations have constant access to His temple, finding safety and protection in the place where God's people meet. He knows that in the altar of God he, too, can find a place that is safe under the protection of God.

As you look at the word portrait of this person, do you see anything that reminds you of yourself? Are you away from the place where you once met God? Perhaps something or someone has intervened and you are exiled from that place. If so, you feel alienated, estranged, debarred, shut out from a real encounter with God. Do you long to come back? Is that longing the most intense thing in your life? It could be. It should be. And the good news is that you can have as much of

God as you intensely want to have. James 4:8 makes the categorical promise, "Come near to God and he will come near to you."

DISCOVERING THE PROCESS

If you set your heart on longing for God, you must be ready for a long journey, a pilgrimage. As a friend said, it is a marathon, not a sprint. Psalm 84 contains three beatitudes, including this encouragement for the journey: "Blessed are those whose strength is in you, who have set their hearts on pilgrimage." We often worry about a good beginning in the Christian life. But the gospel puts just as much emphasis on a good finish. If you long to know God, get ready for a long journey, not a quick fix.

In verses 6 and 7 of Psalm 84, the psalmist paints a picture of your inward, spiritual journey to know God as if it were a pilgrimage from a distant place to the temple in Jerusalem. Such a journey for an actual pilgrim to Jerusalem was a fatiguing, trying experience. Yet the closer the travelers came to the temple, the faster they went. The psalmist assures you that the journey to know God is like that.

Along this journey to Jerusalem the pilgrims pass through the Valley of Baca to make it to a place of springs. The word "Baca" refers to the balsam tree which likes to grow in arid, dry places. Thus the psalmist pictures a long trek through a waterless, barren valley, a terrible wilderness, an arid area. Likewise, not every moment on the way to know God is full of joy and light. All of us have to walk through the Valley of Baca. It can be any of many things. It may be an illness, a time of severe temptation, a period of reversal in our business, an emotional trauma. There is no route to God without crossing the Valley of Baca. And yet an amazing thing happens there. You can dig down through the arid valley floor and find springs. The impossible becomes possible. Affliction can be turned into joy, hardship can be turned into rejoicing, and weakness can be turned into strength.

50

"Consider it pure joy, my brothers, whenever you face trials of many kinds, because you know that the testing of your faith develops perseverance" (James 1:2). That is the possibility for a Christian. He or she can drill right down through the dry place and find living water. I am reminded of this when I think of a dear friend who lost his wife after her five-year battle with cancer. Yet he said that those five years were the best they experienced together. This loving couple dug right down into hardships and found blessings.

During your journey back to God, you will find the sudden blessings that God alone can provide. The pilgrim makes his way across the wasteland of the Judean desert. He is tired, hot, fatigued, weary, about to quit. Suddenly a cloud appears, there is the smell of rain on the desert, and across his dust-caked face the refreshing streaks of rain fall. The psalmist wrote that "the autumn rains also cover it with pools."

Then, as he makes his way toward Jerusalem, a miracle takes place. The desert floor begins to bloom. Israel gets about ten inches of rain per year, and the desert floor reaches a temperature of 190 degrees Fahrenheit on a summer day. Unless the rainfall is perfectly timed, the seeds of flowers can lay dormant for a century. But once every fifty years, the time and amount of rain is right, and the dormant seeds sprout.

In the winter of 1979–1980 this very thing happened. An estimated three thousand to four thousand seeds per square yard grew to maturity. The people who witnessed the miracle saw the floor of the desert literally spring to life with wild flowers. They saw the impossible become possible, the unreal become real. By the intervention of God, the dry place became a place suddenly bursting with beauty. This is always the possibility for God's people as they pass through the dry places.

This very moment, more people than you may think are walking through dry places on their journey back to God. Difficulties, depression, despair, losses, crosses, trials, and tests have dried out their lives. If you are one of these wandering pilgrims, hear the word of God. Then comes a moment when from wells beneath you and the sky above you God will again pour out His presence. Your life will be like an oasis, transformed by faith from the worst place in your life to the best place, from the worst moment to the best moment. It means to believe the words of Jesus Christ, "Whoever believes in me, . . . streams of living water will flow from within him" (John 7:38).

Longing for God also generates renewed resources, as the psalmist writes: "They go from strength to strength." Here is the paradox of faith—different from any other human strength. On a physical journey, the further you go, the weaker you get. Vision dims, hearing weakens, the step falters. Faith demonstrates its might precisely at the point where human strength breaks down. With faith, the nearer the goal, the stronger the pull. It is the mighty truth of Isaiah 40:31: "Those who hope in the Lord will renew their strength. They will soar on wings like eagles; they will run and not grow weary, they will walk and not be faint." And it is the splendid truth of 2 Corinthians 3:18, "We . . . are being transformed into his likeness with ever-increasing glory, which comes from the Lord."

We all admire those physical athletes who have the ability to pace themselves so that the end of the race is even faster than the beginning. A prime example is Harry (Butch) Reynolds, Jr., who could become the fastest runner ever to run around the outdoor track. He had the natural ability to break the epic 400-meter record of 43.86 seconds set in 1968 by Lee Evans at the Mexico City Olympics. His six-foot-three-inch, 177-pound frame takes a monstrous eight-and-a-half-foot stride. His secret is that he runs at 80 percent most of the way, but 95 percent at the close of the race as he rounds the turn toward the tape. The closer to the goal he is, the faster he can run. Going back to God can be just that way. He sustains us with more and more resources the closer we come to the goal.

God makes this promise to you. Whatever else may fail you in your pilgrimage, the life of faith does not. It can indeed move from strength to strength. Dare to believe it and act on it. This is the glory of the Christian faith. When friends, family, companions, health, strength, and opportunity all appear to be gone, you can still move from strength to strength. Like Moses at 120, Abraham at 175, Paul imprisoned in Rome writing his letters, and John on Patmos at 90 writing the Revelation, you can experience the best after the longest time on the journey. The best can be the last!

REVIVAL WITH GOD

Your longing for an encounter with God will not be disappointed. No basic hunger in human life is unmet by God. One who has the ambition to know God (vv. 1–4), and takes the journey to approach God (vv. 5–8), will experience arrival with God, as the psalmist describes in the final stanza of Psalm 84. He is at the place where finally he meets with God. This final arrival leads to a contrast and a confession. He confesses that time in God's presence is better than any other time: "Better is one day in your courts than a thousand elsewhere." Can you confess that the time you experience with God is better than any other time?

The psalmist goes on to describe the place of God's presence: "I would rather be a doorkeeper in the house of my God than dwell in the tents of the wicked." He would rather be a beggar at the gate of the temple in the burning sunshine than live in the sumptuous ease of the tents of the wicked. He prefers the lowest place with God to the highest place without God.

Henri J. Nouwen compared this attitude with that of many people today:

Those who think that they have arrived, have lost their way. Those who think they have reached their goal, have missed it. Those who think they are saints, are demons. An important part of the spiritual life is to keep longing, waiting, hoping, expecting. In the long run, some voluntary

53

penance becomes necessary to help us remember that we are not yet fulfilled. A good criticism, a frustrating day, an empty stomach, or tired eyes might help to reawaken our expectation and deepen our prayer: Come, Lord Jesus, come.

Henri J. Nouwen, *The Genesee Diary*
(New York: Doubleday and Company, 1981),
quoted in Bob Benson and Michael W. Benson,
Disciplines for the Inner Life
(Nashville: Generoux/Nelson, 1989), p. 54

On the journey back to God we are always leaving, always going, always arriving. But our arriving must be with the aching sense that there is still another arrival ahead. Come back—but spend a lifetime on the journey.

Part II

Coming Home to God

"The kingdom of heaven is like treasure hidden in a field. When a man found it, he hid it again, and then in his joy went and sold all he had and bought that field.

"Again, the kingdom of heaven is like a merchant looking for fine pearls. When he found one of great value, he went away and sold everything he had and bought it."

Matthew 13:44–46

6

Treasure Hunt:
Finders and Seekers

Almost everyone likes stories of hidden treasure. In the early 1800s Charles IV King of Spain, whose estate included a precious collection of antique clocks as well as the crown jewels of Spain, knew that Napoleon was about to invade his country. In one room of the palace, he had the clocks walled in. In another room, he had the crown jewels walled in. A faithful servant kept samples of the draperies of both rooms to remember which of the 365 rooms of the palace contained the treasures.

Sure enough, Napoleon conquered Spain and installed his brother Joseph on the throne. In 1814, when Charles's son Ferdinand VII recovered the throne, of course he wanted to find the crown jewels. Every king needs his crown! The faithful servant brought back the swatches of cloth from the draperies. The only problem was that Joseph had changed all the draperies in the palace! Ferdinand was faced with tearing the walls out of 365 rooms—or writing off his loss. He wrote it off. The whole story was considered a legend until a few decades ago, when plumbers found the collection of clocks. It is probable that somewhere in the walls of the palace the crown jewels of Spain are just waiting to be discovered. Someday someone will have the surprise of a lifetime, discovering hidden treasure. (*Smithsonian*, October 1983, p. 140)

Jesus told two stories about coming back to God, comparing this return with finding hidden treasure. Jesus often spoke of "the kingdom of God," simply meaning the rule of God in a person's life. Other times, He referred to "the kingdom of heaven." In Jesus' stories, the kingdom of heaven means ordering your life according to the ideals and character of Jesus. "Thy kingdom come" equals "thy will be done." Some are surprised to return to the kingdom of God; they find it as an unexpected treasure. Others seek the highest good in life and find the kingdom of God. Whether you are a surprised finder or a serious seeker, you must risk everything for the unique opportunity of knowing God's will in your life.

Each of Jesus' parables presents a past picture and tells a timeless truth. Let's look at the picture half and the truth half of these stories to understand how we come back to the rule of God in our life.

FINDING UNEXPECTED TREASURE

This parable presents a past picture, telling of a man who suddenly finds what he is not seeking at all—treasure. A poor day laborer plows the field of another man. The sun sears his back; the simmering soil burns his feet. Just to finish the day is his goal; all he wants is to take his denarius and go home. Suddenly the plow strikes a strange object. The animals jump, the plowman awakes from his half-sleep. He claws at the ground with his hand to find an earthenware jug. Tearing off the top, he sees bright yellow gold. He steals a glance in all directions; no one has seen. He throws some dirt over the jar, runs to the landlord and tells him that he must leave work immediately. By law he was not required to tell the owner of his find, for it had been buried years before by ancient Amorites. Transported by joy, in a state of delirious exultation, he knows that his whole life is about to change. He immediately sells everything he has and buys the field—which would have been a good value for what he paid. But he forgets the field; he has the treasure.

Hidden treasures today are rare. In the ancient biblical lands, however, they were common. Palestine, caught as a land bridge between Egypt and the great empires, was repeatedly invaded, ravaged, and captured. Multitudes buried gold. There were no banks. The government, nobility, clergy, and Arab invaders all robbed the common people often and without warning. Because of this, the people quickly buried treasure in the ground, in walls, in tree trunks, or wherever they could. Earthquakes could cover up entire cities and bury gold with them. All kinds of people quickly buried what they had in the face of invasion or political change. They left, they died, they were captured, and no one knew where the treasure was hidden.

W. M. Thompson was a missionary in Syria and Palestine for thirty years. He told of workmen digging up a garden in Sidon. They found several copper pots of gold. They did exactly like the man in the parable—concealed their find with care. But then, wild with joy, they could not keep their mouths shut. The governor of the city caught them, and recovered two of the pots, and it was found that they contained eight thousand pure gold coins of Alexander and his father Philip. Thompson saw hundreds of persons all over the country spending their last penny looking for such treasure. Until this century, finding buried treasure was the ancient working man's equivalent hope of winning the lottery today.

Such stories of plowmen finding treasures have historical basis. The rabbis told of a man whose ox suddenly sank into the ground as he was plowing. The ox had fallen into a treasure trove which became the property of the happy plowman.

Jesus' parable tells a timeless truth. Many find the rule of God in their lives without seeking. They stumble onto joy.

By accident, by sudden revelation, by a sunburst of unexpected light, Jesus Christ invades their life. Their experience is recorded in Romans 10:20: "'I was found by those who did not seek me; I revealed myself to those who did not ask for me.'"

The Bible is full of people who suddenly encountered the ultimate treasure of God's invasion of their lives. It included the shepherds watching their flocks by night, who were suddenly surprised by a multitude of the heavenly angels singing to them. You can rest assured they were not sitting around Bethlehem's pastures expecting a concert by a thousand angels! But suddenly it happened. All they wanted was to keep their toes from freezing off in the winter wind and to keep the wolf from snatching their sheep. All they wanted was to find the meager grass in the rocky soil. But suddenly angels sang to them. They found an unexpected treasure.

A woman of Samaria found an unexpected treasure at Jacob's well at noon, when she went there alone. Other women always went in the cool of the day, but she went at noon, in the heat, alone. Ashamed. The Jews rejected the Samaritans as half-breeds. She was a Samaritan rejected by other Samaritans. On a hot day she wanted some cold water for her hot tongue; but she went alone because her hot passions had ruined her life. Then she met Jesus beside the well. She came looking for water to drink; but she left with the water of life. John adds the detail that she left her water pot at the well and ran to tell others. Just like the plowmen who eagerly sold his cup, cloak, and whatever else because of the joy of the find, she left her water pot. She found unexpected treasure.

The jailer in Philippi had just gone to sleep. It had been a hard day at the jail. After two preachers caused a riot, he had finally gotten them into stocks—and then they started singing in the middle of the night. He had just gone to sleep when the whole earth shook. In light of Roman law, he was ready to kill himself if his prisoners escaped. Then Paul told him how to rescue more than his prisoners, how to save his very inner life. The jailer got all shook up when the jail shook down, but he found hidden treasure.

Did you stop looking for hidden treasure in God a long time ago—stop believing that Jesus Christ could add an exciting, different dimension to your life? For some of you it stopped in childhood. Perhaps you remember warm summer days in Vacation Bible School when Jesus seemed to be alive. For others of you the treasure hunt stopped with the cynicism of college years. Some professor told you that the Old Testament was no different from other Semitic books and the New Testament was a patchwork of human invention. Maybe that's when you stopped thinking of Jesus as a life-changing reality. For others, perhaps you lost any expectation of hidden spiritual treasure amidst the demands of a career, or as little compromises dulled your ethics, or because of the constant pull of the material world.

If that's your situation, your whole life now belongs to the ritual rut of the routine. Like the man in the poem, "Morning, evening, afternoon—you measure out your life with coffee spoons." You plow through life the same way every day. You have no expectation at all that your plowshare will strike a treasure.

I have news for you. Today—in a moment—you can find hidden treasure, the rule of Christ in your life. It will cause you to invest everything you are, just to have that treasure. Your life can change suddenly—for the mere joy of it. If you are sitting there thinking, *What does it cost to be a Christian? What do I have to invest?* you've misunderstood the story. The emphasis rests on the great *joy* that seized the plowman. It surpassed all measure; it carried him away. It penetrated his innermost being; everything else lost its value. That he surrendered everything most valuable to him was a matter of course. He was carried away by joy, compelled by joy, in a state of hilarious exultation. The fact that he had to sell his old cup, his cloak, or anything else meant nothing to him.

That means right here, while you read, you can discover hidden treasure. Are you willing to grasp the moment and place everything on the table in order to return to God? There is an element of urgency and risk. The plowman sold everything that he had in order to capture the hidden treasure. Jesus expects you to risk everything in faith in order to come back to God.

SEEKING THE HIGHEST GOD—AND FINDING HIS RULE

Some are surprised at the opportunity to come back to God. Others are seeking fulfillment in life and stumble onto Jesus Christ in the search. This is the meaning of the parable of the pearl merchant.

Even though this is a twin to the parable of the plowman, the picture presented is very different. This is no day laborer plowing a field. Jesus presents a traveling pearl merchant—not a shopkeeper, but a man of business on a grand scale—who traveled to the pearl fisheries of the Persian Gulf or India in search of pearls. He was not a collector, but a dealer. What he bought in the East he could easily sell in the West for vast sums. Here is a man such as few men are. Immediately this picture is different. There were many plowmen in fields, but there were only a few such men as this. He would not be surprised by a treasure; he was looking for it, seeking the very best.

He was seeking excellent pearls, until late in the nineteenth century the most valued of all gems. Diamonds now have replaced them in status; but in biblical times diamonds were so rare as to be unheard of. In the ancient world, Pliny says, Cleopatra had two pearls worth the equivalent of four million dollars. Julius Caesar presented the mother of Brutus with a pearl worth $350,000. So now we have more understanding of this merchant who was seeking pearls. He had great skills to gauge the shape, tint, and smoothness of pearls. And he was worth a fortune.

62

Suddenly he finds even more than he was seeking. He finds one pearl of great value, a pearl above all others. One can almost imagine the setting in the Middle East. He contacts a sheik of the pearl trade and is invited to the sheik's grand tent. After many pleasantries and obligatory greetings, he is taken further into the tent. Then the sheik produces a silken purse. Out of it he palms a pearl of perfect proportion.

There is a quickening of breath as his eyes meet the pearl merchant's. Immediately the pearl merchant must have it. The emphasis rests on the suddenness of his possession. At once he sold everything that he had. The purchase cost him the possessions of a long career. That means that he not only traded all the other pearls that he had, but also everything else. He liquidated every asset that he had. He recognized that he found something beyond price. It was as it is with the Hope Diamond. Twice the 44.5-carat diamond was taken from the Smithsonian Museum. It went once to the Louvre and once to South Africa. Both times it was insured for a million dollars—but the money meant nothing. You cannot place a value on an irreplaceable object. The pearl merchant knew that. He had found something beyond value.

Such incredible love of a pearl is not without example today. In 1917 New York socialite May C. Plant traded a house on Fifth Avenue for a pearl necklace valued at one million dollars. In 1905, when Ceylon announced the opportunity to fish in a new pearl fishery, forty thousand gem dealers, divers, and others descended on Manaar. In six weeks five thousand divers retrieved eight-one million oysters. Only two oysters out of a thousand contain a natural, round pearl. When Jesus' pearl merchant found a pearl above all others, he had found a rare thing in the earth.

The day laborer had been surprised by treasure. The pearl merchant found what he had always been seeking.

This parable tells a timeless truth. There are those actively seeking the best things in life: meaning, purpose, reality, escape from futility and frustration. Maybe you're one of these people, seeking a sense of well-being in high and honorable ways. You seek it in work, but work becomes a stern taskmaster which yields no ultimate meaning. You seek it in human love, but even that does not fill the void in your heart. You seek it as physical discipline and become the master of your body in diet and exercise; but that does not fill the emptiness. You seek it in learning, and you accumulate degrees; but that does satisfy. You seek it in position and power over others; but that is like saltwater—the more you drink such power, the more power you want. Every one of these examples may be a pearl—but not the pearl you really want. Your reach always exceeds your grasp. You almost touch it but you do not have it. It is like chasing your shadow.

In contrast, Jesus promises that seekers can be finders. The Gospel of Luke includes the story of Anna and Simeon, two very old, tired seekers, waiting in the temple for years to see the Messiah. They became finders, held the baby Jesus, blessed God, and went on to eternity. Seekers do find. The Ethiopian eunuch had traveled to Jerusalem to learn the Jewish law and enter the Jewish temple—two pearls in their own way. But on the way home the seeker became the finder. He met Philip, who explained to him how the prophecy had been fulfilled. Philip baptized the eunuch and he "went on his way rejoicing.

Similarly, Lydia, the seller of purple, went to the riverside at Philippi, because that is where Jews gathered to seek God in the absence of a synagogue of ten men. As she listened to Paul's message there, "the Lord opened her heart." Because she sought, she found. The greatest Christian theologian of the early church sought everywhere. Augustine of North Africa, who tried every philosophy of his day, found the pearl of pearls in Christ. C. S. Lewis lost something he called joy in his boyhood and sought it for a lifetime—until he found it in Christ.

There are certainly searchers reading this, pearl merchants of the inner life. This could be the end of your search.

Jesus Christ meets you today. You can hand to Him every other pearl and have the one you've looked for.

But some will not. You would rather have paste pearls than the real one. Spiros Zodhiates tells of a young couple on a fast track in their social life. As the season approached, they went to the social matriarch of their city, an old friend, and asked her to loan the ambitious young woman her priceless necklace of perfect, natural pearls. After some thought, the matriarch of society loaned the pearls for the duration of the season. The very first night they were stolen. But more than that, the young couple on the fast track knew that their life's ambitions for fame, visibility, and social prominence were gone with the pearls. In a panic, they flew to a distant emporium, described the necklace to a master jeweler, and had the strand recreated. It cost them everything they would ever have. At the end of the season, they presented the matron with the replacement necklace.

It ruined their entire lives. At enormous cost they paid for years. When the older woman was about to die, out of guilt the young woman went to her bedside. She confessed the whole charade. The older woman shrieked from her bed: "You fool! Those were paste pearls. No one ever loans the real ones. You've wasted your life for paste pearls."

Be careful that you don't come to the end of the way only to realize you have worked, learned, loved, and played for paste pearls.

TAKING THE RISK

The similarities between the finder and seeker outweigh any differences. In these parables, Jesus again argues from the lesser to the greater. If a day laborer will dispossess himself of everything he has in order to have a worldly treasure, how much more should we risk everything for the kingdom of God? If a shrewd merchant can value one pearl so highly that he is willing to commit everything he has to its purchase, how much more highly should we value the kingdom of God and risk everything to have it?

It is exactly the opposite of the excuses given by those invited to the king's banquet described in the parable in Matthew 22. So urgent is the opportunity presented that Jesus says we are to cut off hands that get in its way (Matt. 5:30), let the dead bury their dead while we follow Him (Matt. 8:22), and leave parents and family (Matt. 10:37). This is no lame, same, tame Savior calling for modernized, trivialized, bargain-basement, discount religion. We are to risk everything for the kingdom of God.

What does "everything" mean? Does it mean that we must literally sell out, liquidate? No, for Jesus did not ask everyone to do that. But it does mean that we should be willing to give up everything that prevents God's rule in our lives. Relationships, businesses, hobbies, property—if it prevents God's rule in our lives, out it goes.

You will find then that life is like another parable from another land. A blind Indian beggar sat beside a road, fingering the rice in his little bowl. Wearing only a loin cloth, he sat in poverty beside a road that stretched into nowhere both ways. The scarce travelers occasionally gave him a little rice. One day he heard the thunder of a chariot in the distance. It was the grand entourage of the maharajah. This was a moment that had never come before. Surely the great one would stop and give him baskets of rice.

Indeed, the golden chariot of the maharajah stopped before the poor beggar. The great one stepped down and the beggar fell before him. Then the sky seemed to fall in. "Give me your rice," said the great one. A fearful, hateful, scowl masked the face of the beggar. He reached into his bowl and thrust one grain of rice toward the maharajah. "Is that all?" said the great one. The beggar spat on the ground, cursed, and threw him one more grain of rice. The great one turned, entered his chariot, and was gone.

The beggar—angry, empty, and crushed—fingered the remaining rice he had hoarded in his bowl. He felt something hard, different from the rice. He pulled it out. It was one grain of gold. He poured out his rice, caring nothing for it now. He found one other grain of gold. Had he trusted the great one, he could have had a grain of gold for every grain of rice.

So it is with Christ. You purchase the kingdom—you come back to God—by giving your grains of rice for His grains of gold. Why not come back now? You win in the exchange.

"Even now," declares the Lord,
  "return to me with all your heart,
    with fasting and weeping and mourning."

Rend your heart
  and not your garments.
Return to the Lord your God,
  for he is gracious and compassionate,
slow to anger and abounding in love,
  and he relents from sending calamity.
Who knows? He may turn and have pity
  and leave behind a blessing—
grain offerings and drink offerings
  for the Lord your God.

Joel 2:12–14

7

Come Back Now!

Most of us love to hear stories of return, accounts of how somebody came back again. Amando Munoz, a wiry migrant worker from Texas, was picking tomatoes on a farm near Lake Worth, Florida, when Immigration officials swooped down, demanding his papers; but he had lost his billfold. Even though he was a U. S. citizen living in Harlingen, Texas, he could not prove it. Along with twelve others, he was taken to the Miami airport and flown to the nearest point in Mexico, on the Yucatan Peninsula. He was dumped out of the plane, twelve hundred miles from his home and family, with only ten dollars in his pocket.

In an incredible odyssey, he worked and walked his way toward Mexico City. There he nearly froze at night while it took two whole days to walk across the city. Then it was another six hundred miles across the country. The only thing that kept him going was the thought of not seeing his mother again.

After two months he reached Matamoras, where he called his fifty-three-year-old mother, a cleaning woman with six children. His nineteen-year-old sister, a senior at Harlingen High School, brought his papers. He told his mother, "Don't cry,

Mama. I'm back." His mother said, "Let me cry." ("Amando Comes Home," *Time*, 19 February 1973, p. 26)

Stories of a return like that move all but very cynical and hard hearts. There is something about coming back that speaks to the deepest feelings in all of us. We all long to get back home again. In no area of life is this more pressing that the desire to get back to God. When we are away from God, we do not feel comfortable. When we are alienated from God, we do not feel at home with ourselves or with others. Is there a way back?

Tucked away toward the end of the Old Testament is the book of Joel. Although it is referred to as "minor prophecy," there is nothing minor about the prophet Joel as he describes coming back to God. The theme of his prophecy is that you can come back to God, even though it seems too late. Joel gives hope, but avoids presumption, because he does not say you can *always* come back. The door is open now; it will shut later.

No book in the Bible has a more unified, simple theme. Joel said that judgment, in the form of a locust plague, was already moving toward God's people who had gone away from Him. The people had two choices. Even at the last moment they could return to God. If they chose not to return, they would face God Himself in the form of the locust plague.

It's hard to imagine the reality of a locust plague in the biblical world. I remember a plague of crickets that came and went in Texas when I was a boy. They made a mess, but they left. A biblical locust plague, on the other hand, created permanent devastation. There were such plagues in Palestine in 1845, 1865, 1892, 1899, 1904, and in 1915, the worst of all. That was the year a loud noise was heard before the locusts were seen. The sun was suddenly darkened. Showers of their excrement fell from the air. The government issued a proclamation in April of that year, requiring every man sixteen to sixty years old to gather eleven pounds of locust eggs daily and deliver them to the officials. Every leaf was gone from every plant and the bark was pealed from every tree. The fields were stripped. Arab babies left beneath a tree were devoured before their screams were heard. In Palestine, a locust plague means disaster.

The prophet Joel saw such a judgment coming immediately upon the people: "The day of the Lord is great and very terrible; and who can endure it?" (2:11). Yet even at the last moment he assured them that they could return to God before life was devoured. As the locusts descended, God cried, "Even now return to me. . . ."

Do you think you have been away from God so long that you could never come back? Do you have a vague sense of dread that something is about to happen to you unless you return to God? If so, you recognize that physically, psychologically, and spiritually you are about to hit the wall—unless you come back. Inwardly, a plague of unseen emotional locusts is eating up your inner life. The green leaf of hope is gone and the sunlight of God's presence is eclipsed.

But there is good news. You can come back now. You can return this very moment. You can come back to God—not because of your performance, but because of His character. He is the Father who always welcomes you back home.

RETURNING WITH INWARD INTENSITY

The Bible abounds with invitations to return to God. If you think God does not desire you to return, you have never understood the Book. The prophet cries, "Even now return. . . ." The word "return" is one of the great words in all the Old Testament. It means a total reorientation of life back toward God. In his farewell address Moses foresaw that God's people Israel would later abandon God; but he also saw that they would return: "When you and your children return to the Lord . . . God will restore your fortunes" (Deut. 30:2). At the same time Moses foretold their leaving, he told them they could return!

When Solomon dedicated his temple, he too knew that God's people would someday leave the living God: "If they

71

turn back to you with all their heart and soul . . . hear their prayer" (1 Kings 8:48). God acknowledged Solomon's prayer.

The stern prophet Amos reminded God's people of everything God had done to them to drive them back to Himself. Their stomachs were empty, rain did not fall, blight and insects devoured their crops, disease and war took their sons, cities fell—yet three times, God cries, "you have not returned to me." Amos pleaded that everything God had done to them was in order that they might return; but they did not do so (Amos 4:6–11).

If you are away from God, all of His activity in your life is in order that you return to Him. There is not a detail in the life of a person alienated from God that He does not wish to use to drive you back to Himself. Illness, accident, financial disaster, family loss, and a thousand other things are God's pleading push that you return to Him. That is the call of the prophet Joel: "even now . . . return" (2:12).

But that word cannot stand alone. Returning to God is not a casual matter. Joel adds: "with all your heart," indicating the entire force of your moral purpose. It is a phrase of intensity. For us, the heart is connected only with affection. In the Bible the heart is more connected with the mind of intellect and the resolve of will. It is a word of totality and intensity. You cannot come back unless you come back with all your heart.

It is always fascinating to read of wholehearted human endeavor—amazing stories of total dedication. For example, the U.S. Marines conduct a supersecret sniper program in Quantico, Virginia. The school admits twenty-five men for a eight-week course of sixteen-hour days. Very few pass. To graduate, each goes on a mock mission into a well-defined area where instructors search for the sniper. If they can find him, they can fail him.

To get in range of the target, a sniper may move forward at a rate of one inch per hour. He may sit for days absolutely still, despite cold, rain, insect bites, and fear. No one gets out without singleness of heart. ("School for Snipers," *U.S. News and World Report*, 21 April 1986, p. 62) We expect that kind of intensity from Olympic champions, concert pianists, doctoral candidates, and everyone else at the highest levels of human achievements. Likewise, God expects it when we come back to Him. God deserves singleness of heart because He is God! Most of us intend to come back to God—sometime. But we fail because our intention never becomes intense.

Returning to God requires inward reality, not just outward ceremony: "Rend your heart and not your garments" (2:13). That is the biblical way of saying, "the external is not enough." In the biblical world, to tear a garment was the ultimate, outward expression of returning to God. It expressed exceptional emotion on the occasion of overwhelming misfortune. In the Bible, one tore his garments before putting on the sackcloth of mourning. The sackcloth was a coarsely woven garment of black goat's hair that covered only a man's loins. It left the chest free for beating in repentance. This was the ultimate outward symbol of returning to God.

Jacob tore his garments when he thought his son Joseph was slain (Gen 37:34). Joshua and Caleb tore their clothes at the lost opportunity to enter the promised land (Num. 14:6). David and all his army tore their clothes when they heard of the death of Saul and Jonathan (2 Sam. 1:11). If I were to rip open my shirt in the pulpit, pop off the buttons, tear away my tie, and throw off my coat, the congregation would think, *that is really intense!* But such outwardness is not intense enough.

I suppose the most famous, outward repentance in history was performed by Henry IV in January 1077. Henry was the Holy Roman Emperor, the most powerful political figure in the world. He had been deposed and excommunicated by Pope Gregory. After two months of waiting, he appeared at Canossa, an impregnable fortress on the northern slope of the Apennines. The winter of 1077 was one of the coldest in all history. Begging the pope to restore him to the church, the emperor stood from the twenty-fifth to the twenty-eighth of January in the court between the inner walls as a penitent, with bare head and bare feet. He knocked at the door in vain for entrance. The stern old pope, as hard as rock and cold as snow, refused entrance for three days. When the inner gate was finally opened, the king entered. In the prime of his life, he was the heir of crowned monarchs, a man of tall and noble presence; but he threw himself at the feet of the pope, an old man of small and unimpressive stature. He burst into tears and cried, "Spare me, holy father, spare me." Even the onlookers were moved to tears to see the Holy Roman Emperor so humiliate himself externally. Yet in spite of that act, there is no evidence that Henry was changed or born again, or that his life was revolutionized in spite of all his outward penitence. (Philip Schaff, *History of the Christian Church*, pp. 53–55)

To stand in the snow in freezing weather without shoes or hat is the maximum in external religious demonstration. God is not impressed with such a show. He wants *inward* intensity.

We modern American Christians have our equivalent outward acts. When we are away from God, we can decide to go back to church, to Bible study, or to prayer meeting; we can sing louder, give more, visit more, do more. But all of that can mean nothing inwardly. Joel cries to an outwardly religious generation, "Rend your heart." Tear your heart, crush your heart, crack your heart. Make it penetrable, pervious, soft, warm, moldable. And just as did the adulterous David, you will find that God returns to a broken and crushed heart (Ps. 51:17).

There is actually a hardness scale, on which talc is 1, fingernail is 2½, window glass is 5, and diamond is 10. (*Guiness Book of World Records*, 1988, pp. 171, 181) If there were a scale of the hardness or softness of the human heart, where would your heart fall? If you want to come back to God, you must change inwardly. You must have a heart than can be rent, torn, softened, and penetrated.

But there is also an outwardness in turning to God, to be expressed to the maximum degree that is compatible with your personality. A return to God may involve a fast, for instance—a voluntary abstention from a food or a physical relationship or activity in order to concentrate on God. In our day, a fast could include turning off the television, radio, stereo, or telephone, and shutting up ourselves with God.

Joel adds the words "weeping and mourning." These words should not be lightly treated. When you have been away from God, you must emote your feelings when you return. Christians must not only be right thinkers doctrinally, they must be deep feelers emotionally. Your emotions are the handles by which your faith grips you. To be a Christian, you must feel deeply the emotions of gratitude, holy fear, joy, and love. Holy fear is not terror, but it is respect, humility, and grief over one's sin.

An effervescent woman wandered into a liturgical service. As the pastor preached, she echoed his words with a loud, "Praise the Lord!" Another woman leaned over to say, "Excuse me, but we don't praise the Lord in this church." A man down the aisle corrected her, "Yes we do; it's on page 19." When you come back to God, you must feel more than what's printed on page 19 in a formal book of liturgy! Your feelings must be so intense, they are printed on your heart.

There is something about any return that moves the deepest emotions within us. The Atlantic salmon is more than a fish; it moves humankind—inspires, mystifies, and intrigues us. It can vault six feet into the air and swim up a waterfall. But most of all, we are intrigued by the salmon because it returns. After traveling the ocean, it surfaces as a sudden, subtle shimmering something seen in the sunlit stream where it was spawned.

In 1985 the Newton, Kansas High School had the grandest reunion in history. More than four thousand alumni representing seventy-five years of classes descended on the little town. It caught the heart of the nation. Why? Because so many had returned after years away. ("Yes, You Can Go Home Again to the Great High School Reunion," *U.S. News and World Report*, 8 July 1985, p. 53)

And who could forget February 1973, when the first Vietnam POWs walked off the airplane at Clark Air Force Base in the Philippines? I still remember the tears in my eyes as those gaunt, pale, dignified, triumphant men walked off the plane. Why did it move us? Because they had returned.

There is a reason why we respond this way to returns of all kinds. That reason is the desire down deep in our own hearts to get back to God. Every other kind of return simply reminds us that we need to get back to God. If fish, high school students, and soldiers can go home, why can't you come home to God? You can. The door is opened from His side.

DIVINE INTEGRITY

On January 7, 1980, Katheleen drove her daughter Wavie to Citrus High School in Inverness, Florida. It was the last time she would see Wavie for a long time. When the sixteen-year-old daughter did not return from school that day, Katheleen and her husband Jesse sought help from the police, the FBI, the governor, and even from national TV networks. Jesse and Katheleen, working people, were not about to give up. They printed thousands of fliers and delivered stacks of bulletins to truck stops across Florida and Georgia. Thousands of people responded. Some said they saw her. Exhausting many of their resources, they never gave up. On Tuesday, June 29, 1982 they received a call that located Wavie in Twin Cities, Georgia. By six o'clock the next morning, Wavie's parents were in the tiny Georgia town, overjoyed at finding their daughter.

Later, Wavie told her story. She really had not intended to run away from home. But on that January day, friendly strangers had offered her a ride to a nearby truck stop—and then on to Georgia. The farther she got away from home, the more frightened she was of being punished for leaving. Each hour away from home made it harder to return. She feared the reunion. Dozens of times she had dialed her parents' phone number, but hung up in panic before they answered. She had written hundreds of letters to her parents—but never mailed them. She was afraid of returning home at the very same time her parents were exhausting all of their resources to find her. (Gary Turbak, "Return of a Runaway Child," *Reader's Digest*, November 1982, pp. 97–102)

Isn't that the way we feel when we have been away from God? We recognize He wants us back; but we fear the encounter, even while God employs all His resources in Calvary's love seeking us. There is no need to fear the reunion. You can come back now.

Four aspects of God's character encourage you to return (Joel 2:13).

First, God is "gracious." This particularly refers to the goodwill of a superior to an inferior person. God condescends. He stoops all the way down from His throne to a cross. He wanted you back so much that He sent His own Son to bleed to death on a stick of wood—for you.

Second, God is "compassionate." This word comes right out of a home. In Hebrew the word suggests a father or mother concerned about a sick child. God is like that. How does He look at us when we are away from Him? He watches us like a parent who tenderly cares for a child threatened with a high fever. Jesus demonstrated the compassion of God, even to the point of death for His children.

Third, God is "slow to anger." One little boy was asked in Sunday school, "What does the wrath of God mean?" The youngster responded, "It means that God got mad and stayed mad." Not so, says the prophet. His word suggests someone who takes a deep breath in order to postpone and place at a distance any expression of anger. Jesus did not come into the world to condemn the world but to rescue the world (John 3:17). From the Cross Jesus cries out, "I am not angry with you. I want you back."

Best of all, God is "abounding in love." Every kindness of God in your life is a reminder that He wants you back. He does not desire to drive you back to Himself with a whip. Instead, "God's kindness leads you towards repentance" (Romans 2:4). When you leave God, you must trample under foot mountains of His kindness, because everything good in your life comes from His hand—family, work, health, friendship, church, and a thousand other things. Each of these calls, "Come back, now."

Not many people remember what happened at Stark, New Hampshire from the spring of 1944 to the spring of 1946. Some 250 German prisoners of war were imprisoned there. Camp Stark was a hard place. Part of the punishment was cutting pulpwood in the nearby rocky hills. Most of the prisoners were boys, eighteen or nineteen years old. All but the hardiest were beaten down by the hard work. Although there was no vindictiveness, there were guards, barbed wire, and bad memories.

But Allen Koop, a college history professor, did an unusual thing a few years ago. He tracked down the long-ago prisoners and invited them back to the camp. In their sixties, the German former prisoners came back to the place where they had been prisoners forty years earlier. There the prisoners and their guards were reunited in an act of forgiveness and reunion. (John Skow, "In New Hampshire: An Unusual Reunion," *Time*, 3 November 1986, pp. 14–15)

Some of us fear prisons of the past and present. God seems far away. But He calls us back to the very place of our captivity and alienation, then forgives us on the spot. He welcomes us into His fellowship, calling, "Come back, now!"

Now Moses was tending the flock of Jethro his father-in-law,
the priest of Midian, and he led the flock to the far side of the
desert and came to Horeb, the mountain of God. There the
angel of the Lord appeared to him in flames of fire from
within a bush. Moses saw that though the bush was on fire it
did not burn up. So Moses thought, "I will go over and see this
strange sight—why the bush does not burn up."

When the Lord saw that he had gone over to look, God called
to him from within the bush, "Moses! Moses!"
And Moses said, "Here I am."

"Do not come any closer," God said. "Take off your sandals,
for the place where you are standing is holy ground." Then he
said, "I am the God of your father, the God of Abraham, the
God of Isaac and the God of Jacob." At this, Moses hid his face,
because he was afraid to look at God.

God said to Moses, "I AM WHO I AM. This is what you are to say
to the Israelites: 'I AM has sent me to you.'"

Exodus 3: 1-14

Now Moses was tending the flock of Jethro his father-in-law, the priest of Midian, and he led the flock to the far side of the desert and came to Horeb, the mountain of God. There the angel of the Lord appeared to him in flames of fire from within a bush. Moses saw that though the bush was on fire it did not burn up. So Moses thought, "I will go over and see this strange sight—why the bush does not burn up."

When the Lord saw that he had gone over to look, God called to him from within the bush, "Moses! Moses!"
And Moses said, "Here I am."

"Do not come any closer," God said. "Take off your sandals, for the place where you are standing is holy ground." Then he said, "I am the God of your father, the God of Abraham, the God of Isaac and the God of Jacob." At this, Moses hid his face, because he was afraid to look at God.

God said to Moses, "I AM WHO I AM. This is what you are to say to the Israelites: 'I AM has sent me to you.'"

Exodus 3:1–6, 14

8

The Great "I Am"

Fires that burn a large area or burn for a long time have a continuing fascination for most of us. The largest forest fire on record burned 13,500 square miles in East Kalimanton, the Indonesian part of the island of Borneo. The fire burned from February to June 1983, devastating an area bigger than the states of Massachusetts and Connecticut combined.

At the same time in February 1983, a fire storm ravaged southwestern Australia. Winds built to gale force, and within hours, flames raced along miles of coastline. A broad arc of rich farmland and a fragrant eucalyptus forest were quickly reduced to scorched earth. Seventy-five people died, and property damage totaled more than $2.5 billion. There is something awesome about such consuming fires.

But as destructive as these huge fires were, they lacked the power of one small fire that burned more than three thousand years ago on Mt. Sinai. That fire was confined to one desert bush, which burned—but did not burn up. The fire in the bush gave life, not death. And the result of that fire was dedication to God, not destruction.

Moses had been away for forty years when God suddenly called him back to Himself and explained the plan He had for

Moses' life. You can probably identify with some of the reasons Moses had been away from God, as well as the way God invited Moses back.

Meeting God as He Really Is

God moves your life toward a confrontation with Him. You may be moving toward that moment without even knowing it, just as you may not feel yourself moving when you're flying in a jetliner at six hundred miles per hour. God moves you toward Himself. There is a wind blowing, and it carries you in that direction. There is an invisible hand pushing and pulling. When you study Moses' encounter with God, you see clearly how God can spend eighty years leading up to an encounter with Him. Moses moved from being a prince in Egypt to a shepherd in the desert in order to encounter the living God.

God did three things to prepare Moses for an encounter with Himself. In the same way, God will use one or more of these three things in preparing your life for an encounter with Him.

One way God prepares us is with devastating events. Gordon MacDonald calls some of us "broken-world people," those whose worlds have been broken apart, shattered by events. Moses was one of the most striking broken-world people in history. He spent the first forty years of his life in the court of the Egyptian pharaoh, a sun god who lived in and out of his palace in splendor, shining like the sun. The pharaoh did not walk. He was carried in a sedan chair by eight courtiers. As an Egyptian noble, Moses had been bathed, barbered, and pedicured daily. He knew the palace well, a great hall of pillars adorned with lapis lazuli and malachite, and a balcony of gold. Moses had been in what was called "the room of adoration," where only the sons and the nearest friends gathered around the Pharaoh. The princes were brought up in a special part of the palace where they were tutored with friends. It was a life beyond our imagination.

Then suddenly Moses was expelled from the Egyptian court (Exod. 2:15). He literally moved from the palace to the pasture, from the food of royalty to a subsistence diet, from the companionship of nobles to the company of shepherds. One could hardly find a more devastating change of circumstances in world history. Moses spent the next forty years of his life reflecting on the shock, bitterness, and finality of everything he had lost when he was expelled from Egypt. His résumé would have been very simple: "Ex-prince in Egypt, forty years as assistant shepherd to father-in-law." Yet God intended that very devastating experience of loss to set the stages for Moses' confrontation with Him.

Devastating events are part of the fabric of life. You will face them. We all do. They usually come to us in the guise of loss—loss of health, friends, job, opportunity, companions. These losses can make us bitter; they make us want to escape or deny. Or they help us see that a bush is burning with the presence of God on the other side of the devastating event.

The second way God prepares us to return to Him is in isolated places. He sent Moses to the "far side of the desert," farther than he had ever gone before—literally "beyond" or "behind" his customary routes. In the blazing summer the Bedouins leave the low country and go to the high country where the grass grows. When Moses pushed out into the silence of the desert farther than ever before he came to Horeb, which is the name of the region where Mt. Sinai stands. The word "Horeb" means dry, sterile, bleak, and rocky. It was a place of aloneness, isolation, silence, absolute quietness. We can hardly imagine a world this quiet, with no cars running, no faint sound of jets in the air, no television or radio, no sound of children playing or appliances churning. In this quiet place, Moses met God. Not in a crowd, but alone. Not in noise, but in silence. Not in a hurry, but in stillness.

God often pushes those He encounters into great silence. Elijah found a fresh encounter with God not in the busy work of his ministry, but alone in a cave. Jesus encountered God's sustaining power alone in the wilderness. After his Damascus road experience, Paul went into the desert, where he heard the voice of the risen Christ revealing the message he would take to the world.

Do you want to meet God? Prepare in silence. Henri Nouwen writes in *Sojourners* of the need for silence. He recalls the lives of the desert fathers, those monks who fled to the desert for absolute silence. One was named Arsenius, a Roman educator who went to the desert to find God. He prayed, "Lord, lead me into the way of salvation," and heard the response, "Be silent." We are inundated by words. They form the floor, walls, and ceiling of our lives. Words scream at us from radios, TVs, billboards, bumper stickers, and announcements. Nouwen said that while driving through Los Angeles he had had the strange sensation of driving through a dictionary: "use me, take me, buy me, drink me, eat me, smell me, touch me, kiss me, sleep with me." Words gone wild.

He goes on to say that words tangle us up with this world and put out the inner fire within us. Our spiritual life is like a steam bath. When we open the door, the room loses its heat. When we are always talking, the fire of the spirit within us cools. Silence has become a fearful thing. It creates nervousness. Many of us would rather do anything than sit alone with ourselves in an absolutely quiet place.

Thomas a Kempis wrote the immortal devotional classic, *The Imitation of Christ*. In chapter 20 he calls for silence: "The greatest saints avoid the society of men, when they could conveniently, and did rather choose to serve God, in secret."

Do you wish for an encounter with God that changes your life? Fight and flee to find silence. Make this silence a violent obsession. Some of you are now in an enforced silence and isolation. You have no choice. Then thank God, and use that enforced isolation as the preparation to meet Him. Have your own Horeb. Search for your own Sinai. Desire your own desert. Find it at home, or away from home. Find silence if you would find God.

The third way God prepares us to return to Him in humbling activities. At age eighty, Moses did not have anything as his own. Egypt faded in his memory. He felt his own life ebbing away in that wilderness. Dreams of achievement, notoriety, and leadership drained into the sand of the desert. Shock, rejection, and bitterness faded into the desert landscape, along with the feelings in Moses that needed to die: pride, self-sufficiency, impatient impulsiveness.

It is in being humbled that God prepares us to encounter Him. In 1940, at age fifty-four, the world-famous theologian Karl Barth was called up to military service and was given a helmet, uniform, rifle, and bayonet. At his urgent request he was not posted to office work, which his respectful superior wished to do for the world figure. No. Barth stood watch by the Rhine at midnight, and slept on straw. Once a fellow soldier genially asked him if he was ever confused with the famous Professor Barth. Sometimes he preached to them, recalling later, "I learned once again to write a sermon that is really preached at a man." He was thoroughly humbled, and connected God with man in a new way.

Are you humbled? Have you been demoted? Are you less in the eyes of others or yourself than you were? Then God is preparing you to meet Him in that experience, as He did Moses. Do not resent it. Expect God in it.

Remember that Jesus also faced devastation, isolation, and humiliation. His life on earth began with devastation—a trip to Egypt. He grew up in isolation—in Nazareth. He knew the humility of being assistant carpenter to His stepfather. Then suddenly He went to the Jordan. Heaven burst open, God's voice spoke, and the Spirit descended.

Last winter, some of you buried bulbs in the earth. They were hidden in the darkness, the quietness, the isolation of the soil. Suddenly one spring day they burst through the surface in colorful glory. Confronting God happens like that.

EXPERIENCING GOD AS HE REALLY IS

In very few lives does the decisive moment of change happen when it is expected, however. The day Moses heard God's voice in the burning bush was his last day as a shepherd; but when the day began, he did not know it would be the last. This could be the last day of your life without an encounter with God, and you did not pick up this book knowing that. When God takes the initiative in meeting you, you do not expect it, just as Moses that day expected nothing different from the thousands of other days during his forty years of hearing the sheep bleat. Then a bush exploded with fire.

Rationalists and liberal critics at this point like to note that some bushes in the desert exploded with spontaneous combustion in the heat, or that there may have been some natural gas leaking beneath this bush. That misses the point. This common bramble bush, this thorn bush (called seneh) burned—but did not burn up. Moses knew that God sometimes had met the men of old at a tree (Genesis 18:1) and that God had been associated with fire from heaven. But here is a combination of the two—a tree on fire, and inside it, the angel of Jehovah. That expression simply means the visible presentation of God Himself, God's ambassador, even perhaps the Lord Jesus before Bethlehem.

Then there was Moses' decisive moment—"I will go over and see why the bush does not burn up." Spiritual curiosity and spiritual initiative marked that moment. Moses did not yawn, scratch his head, and decide it wasn't worth the energy to walk over to the bush on the hot sand of the desert.

Look carefully at how God prepared Moses for this moment. There was the unwilling expulsion from Egypt—its devastation, isolation, and humiliation. But here is a willing compulsion from Moses. A bush burns—he moves toward it.

God takes the initiative in arresting us. Suddenly a spiritual thorn bush explodes with fire. How many bushes burn with God and you do not look? On a late-night walk, God breathes down your neck—and you turn away. A striking Christian confronts you; you sense glory in the person's presence—but you do not stick like a barnacle to learn the secret. God leaps off the page of a devotional book—but you turn on the TV to get away. Most of us never encounter God as we might because when the bush burns, we turn away to the desert. Browning said, "Earth's crammed with heaven, and every common bush afire with God: But only he who sees takes off his shoes, the rest of us sit around and pick dewberries."

God also takes the initiative in instructing us—by what we see. A humble bramble bush burns, but does not burn up! Here the supernatural God enters into the lower natural creation—and burns within it without burning it up. This is God's way. He burns in your life without burning you out.

There was a word in this for Moses. Here was a bush that burned and burned and burned. Moses could not help but compare himself with that bush. Forty years earlier he had tried to burn for God and had burned himself out. He had felt like a heap of ashes for forty years. Now at the end of his life he finds that God can burn in a man's life—and not burn the man out. God was about to burn in Moses' life from his 80th to his 120th year. He would then die with his eye not dim and his natural force not abated. God would burn in the court of Ramses, burn marching through the sea, burn on the mountain, burn in the desert, burn when the people complained—but not burn up Moses.

Moses also found out that there was nothing exceptional about the bush. As Ian Thomas put it, any old bush will do. God could have said, "Do you see that bush over there? That scruffy, scraggly-looking thing? That bush would have done! Do you see this beautiful bush so shapely and fine? That bush would have done, too." Any old bush will do—any old bush, that is, if God is in the bush.

This is a word for you. This is God's desire for humanity. He desires to enter your life like a fire and burn within your humanity—not to burn in a desert bush, but to burn in *you*. As 2 Corinthians 4:16 triumphantly asserts, "Though outwardly we are wasting away, yet inwardly we are being renewed day by day." This is the apostle Paul burning, but not being burned up.

On November 7, 1989 Billy Graham celebrated his seventy-first birthday. Can this actually be true? Most of us think of him as eternally youthful, full of boundless energy and vision. He preached in 1988 in China and the Soviet Union. Tired? Yes. Health problems? Yes, some potentially serious. Burning? Yes. Burned up? Never!

Consider Billy Graham's father-in-law, Dr. L. Nelson Bell, a missionary surgeon from China. At an advanced age, when many men begin to fossilize, Dr. Bell continued to burn. A world Christian figure, he retired at Montreat, North Carolina, where he would go to the shambles where a drunk lived, sober the man up, and lead him to Christ. Burning in China as a missionary doctor. Burning in retirement as a witness to drunks in a small North Carolina village.

That is the lesson of the bush that burns, but does not burn up. Are you about to burn out? Take a look at this bush!

God also instructs us by what we hear. He calls us by name: "Moses, Moses." Just when we think that God has forgotten our address and area code, He calls us by name. That is what encounter with God is all about. You cannot avoid God when He calls you by name. It is one thing for God to speak to a congregation. It is another thing to know that God has called you by name.

God calls us to come close, but not too close. "Take off your sandals, for the place where you are standing is holy ground." The Hebrews took off their shoes where we would take off our hats. When God is really present, there is fellowship and fear, approach and awe. This ought to keep private devotions and the life of faith in a blaze of anticipation. There is no commonness or boredom in the presence of God. The words, "We are standing on holy ground" must be more than a song. It must be the realization that at any time in the life of faith we may encounter God in an experience that burns before us and changes everything. On the other hand, some of us expect nothing to happen in this life of faith—and we get exactly what we expect.

The result of not responding when the bush burns can be eternal. Jean-Paul Sartre became the leading atheistic existential philosopher of this century. He influenced a disillusioned generation away from God. As a youngster, he had a sense of the presence of God, but turned away. His words from fifty years later are haunted with a sense of lost opportunity to meet and know God. He writes that:

> I maintained public relations with the Almighty, but privately I ceased to associate with Him. Only once did I have the feeling He existed. I had been playing with matches and burned a small rug. I was in the process of covering up my crime when suddenly God saw me. I felt His gaze inside my head and on my hands. I whirled about in the bathroom, horribly visible, a live target. Indignation saved me. I flew into a rage against so crude an indiscretion. I blasphemed. . . .
>
> I have just related the story of a missed vocation: I needed God, He was given to me, I received Him without realizing that I was seeking Him. Failing to take root in my heart, He vegetated in me for a while, then He died. Whenever anyone speaks to me about Him today, I say, with the easy amusement of an old beau who meets a former belle: "Fifty years ago, had it not been for that misunderstanding, that mistake, the accident that separated us, there might have been something between us."

Jean-Paul Sartre,
The Words, pp. 102–103

What an incredible assertion! He saw the bush burn. But he turned away. Now at the end of a lifetime, he looked back to see the moment when God was near and he walked away. When the bush burns, we had best draw near.

KNOWING GOD AS HE REALLY IS

No moment compares with this moment, when God tells us His name. To know someone's name is a powerful thing. It singles them out, takes them out of the masses, links us to them. To know God's name is even more powerful. In the Bible God's name means more than just His I.D. God's name means His character, reputation, ability. Moses knew the names of the Egyptian gods. They were numerous and powerful; they appeared to be awesomely successful. But they dwindle to insignificance before the God who burns in the bush.

God's name means His continuity in history. "I am the God of your father." Eighty years earlier, the father of Moses, whose name was Amram, knew and worshiped this same God who burned in the bush. But more than that, this is the same God who talked to Abraham seven hundred years before Moses, and four thousand years before today. If God spoke to me in the same way, He would say, "I am the God of Henry Newton Selby and Albert C. Gregory, your grandfathers. I am the same." We are not meeting in this generation God No. 2. We are here worshiping the same God that we read about in Exodus. He is the God who keeps His covenant, His promises, His people. "O God our help in ages past / our hope in years to come / our shelter from the stormy blast / and our eternal home. . . . Before the hills in order stood / or earth received her frame / from everlasting thou are God / to endless years the same."

When you submit your life over to Him, you submit your life to One who has a recorded track record of four thousand years.

God's name means His activity as well as His history. Many scholars translate God's name in verse 14 as, "I will be what I will be." This means that God is active and reveals Himself to us only in His relationship with us and His activity in our lives. The name of God is not a password we memorize. It is not a definition in a textbook on theology. I recently read the work of an esteemed theologian who divided God into so many categories in such an elaborate outline that one could hardly remember it. You do not meet God like that. You meet God in the *experience* of Him. He gives Himself to you in an active relationship. "I will be what I will be. I am not going to give myself to you like a dictionary definition. Instead, for the next forty years you will *experience* me—in the pillar of fire, in the manna, in the water from the rock, in my judgment, and my mercy."

But more than history or activity—more than anything else—God's name means His immediacy. He is "I AM." He will not meet you in your past. He does not promise to meet you in the future. He says, "I AM." He only meets you in the razor-thin moment of *now*. We would prefer anything to that. This very moment, as you consider His word, He thunders, "I AM!" If you feel no immediacy, no urgency, no nowness, you will never encounter God as He is. Unless God is known in the immediacy of communion this very moment, He is not known.

You see, God blows apart our human categories to tell us who He is. Nothing in language can contain Him or express Him. He is simply "I AM." You can meet Him through His Son Jesus Christ, who said the same thing: "Before Abraham was born, I am!" (John 8:58).

For the word of God is living and active. Sharper than any double-edged sword, it penetrates even to dividing soul and spirit, joints and marrow; it judges the thoughts and attitudes of the heart. Nothing in all creation is hidden from God's sight. Everything is uncovered and laid bare before the eyes of him to whom we must give account.

Hebrews 4:12–13

9

God's Living,
Powerful Word

Bill Bentley moved to the mountains of southern Mexico near Guatemala in 1938. He went there to translate the Bible into the language of a remote tribe in those mountains, the Tzeltals. His fiancée, Marianna, was serving a neighboring tribe. They went back to Pennsylvania to be married, but six days before the wedding Bill died of a heart attack.

Marianna was crushed. God had called her to go to the Tzeltals with Bill. Now, even without him she would go back. The journey took ten days, five on foot and five on horseback. The Tzeltals lived an awful existence. Poverty, alcoholism, violence, disease, and hopelessness darkened the entire region.

After spending six years there alone, learning the language, Marianna was joined by Florence, a missionary nurse. For the first eight years their work met with suspicion, rejection, and hostility from the Tzeltals; the missionaries were unwanted and misunderstood. But they stuck it out.

By 1965, after more than twenty years, they had completed the translation of the New Testament into two dialects.

Then a miracle took place. More than seventy congregations of Christians grew from the seed they planted. Suspicion became faith, rejection became acceptance, hostility became Christian love. The Tzeltals call God's word "good seed"; it had taken root. Twenty-one years of life by two single women and the Word of God grew. They looked forward to spending the rest of their lives translating the Old Testament.

But then Cameron Townsend came. He told the Tzeltal people about the Paez people in the Andes Mountains in southwestern Colombia. They did not have the Word of God. He asked the two women to go and start the entire process over again. Marianna and Florence said yes, and the Tzeltal people became the sponsor for the two ladies to go to Colombia. For the third time Marianna learned a strange language, and for another twenty-one years she and Florence translated the New Testament.

Then Marianna and Florence went back to the sponsor church in southern Mexico with some of the Paez people. What a reunion that was! Thousands of Tzeltal people lined the way to greet them. In the twenty-one years since they had left, the seventy-two congregations they founded had become 322. When they had left there were six thousand believers. When they returned there were forty-four thousand. One-third of the Tzeltals were practicing Christians. Hallelujah for the Word of God!

What other book could do that? If you left a physics text, a biography of a great man, a collection of short stories, a folio of poetry—could any of those books have done what the Bible did for the Tzeltals? No! Only the Word of God can do that. "For the word of God is living and active . . ." (Heb. 4:12).

Our text speaks of the Word of God. Great theologians have debated whether this means the Person of the Son of God or the written Book of God. Learned men have examined the question endlessly. I relish this debate, because it means that the living Word of God, Jesus, and the written Word of God, the Bible, are so closely joined together that the greatest scholars cannot tell whether our text speaks of one or the other. God incarnated Himself in Jesus Christ and Jesus Christ incarnates Himself in this written revelation. God has so joined together the written Word and the embodied Word that it is impossible to divide them.

When you come back to God, the primary instrument for that reunion is the Word of God. The Bible is your road map back home.

GOD'S WORD LIVES

In the Greek, the first and most emphatic word of our text is the word "living"—*living* is the Word of God. Vibrant, vital, vivacious, moving, multiplying, enlivened, energetic—living!

God's Word is living because it is the Word of the living God—the living Christ. He lives, and therefore this Word lives. Just as my hand lives because it is connected with the source of life in my chest, so the Book lives because it is drenched with the life of the One who makes it live.

When Peter confessed Christ, he confessed Him as the Son of the Living God. Around Peter at Caesarea Philippi were the fetishes and remnants of dead gods. When the others began to forsake Jesus, Peter cried out to Him, "Lord, to whom shall we go? You have the words of eternal life" (John 6:68). Like a man clinging to something for his very life, Peter recognized in the words of Jesus Christ the vehicles of life that would last forever. Jesus said, "The words I have spoken to you are spirit and they are life" (John 6:63). This Book vibrates with life because it is inseparably connected with the life of God Himself. It never decays, decomposes, or disintegrates, because it is alive.

We have in our family the Bible of my paternal great-grandfather, a Texas farmer and Baptist preacher in the nineteenth century. It is tattered with time, burned from a fire, soaked with grease from an accident, and stained by the rains of a storm. But I pick it up to read, and immediately it impacts me with the life that is in it.

This would be true of virtually no other book from my great-grandfather's world. I could pick up a science, mathematics, physics, medical, law, engineering, or any other kind of book from his generation and it would be dead, dated, and surpassed by a thousand other books. I pick up his Bible and Jesus Christ leaps off its pages and confronts me in the same way He does in the newer Bible I hold. The Bible lives because it is the Word of the living God.

On the Spanish galleon *Atocha,* which sank off Key West, Florida in 1622, were four seeds, preserved an unprecedented 365 years in salt water. When planted in a lab, they sprouted and stood three inches tall. Life produces life. God's Word does the same.

The Bible is the *living* Word because it gives life. A living thing is identified as living because it propagates, it gives birth, it multiplies. A thing is alive because it gives life to another. A rock does not give birth to a rock; a brick does not give birth to a brick. A single-celled protozoan and a great blue whale are alive because they give life. How do I know this Book lives? Because it gives life. Peter says it: "For you have been born again, not of perishable seed, but of imperishable, through the living and enduring word of God" (1 Peter 1:23). What other book could have been left among the Tzeltals and given life to forty-four thousand people, then cause them to send two women to Colombia, where it was translated into another remote dialect—giving life to thousands more? Only the Word of God.

This Book has a strange, mystic vitality. It acts toward me like a person. It wrestles with me, smites me, comforts me, smiles on me, frowns on me, clasps my hand, warms my heart, weeps with me, sings with me, whispers to me. This Book never gets sick or old. Its eye never dims, its ear never deafens, its step never slackens, its brow is never creased with a frown. This Book lives, breathes, moves. You do not bring life to Scripture; you *draw* life from it. Even a single verse can give eternal life.

How many times I have come to my study, weary and stressed with the care of the church, distracted by everything having to do with the thousands of people under my pastoral care. My mind has been clouded, my body has been tired. I open my Bible to a passage. I open my Greek testament. I open various translations. Then the strangest thing happens, over and over. The weariness drains out of my body; the distractions leave my mind. Suddenly I am captured, my heart pounds, my eyes widen, my mind leaps to life. Nothing does that to me except the Word of God.

God's Word lives because it has an inherent energy. When Jesus was arrested, a word from Him forced His adversaries to the ground (John 18:6). Similarly, Christ will win His final victory over all opposition with His energetic Word alone (Rev. 19:15). The Word of God has an energy that is never without results. It is always full of activity for salvation or for judgment.

Mere human beings have created energy. And in this creation, our nation's ninety-nine nuclear reactors generate thirty tons of highly radioactive material each year. It will take three million years for this radioactive waste to decay to the point that it is no longer a threat. Some of this material is so energetic that it boils by itself for five years. It is so energetic that nothing we know can hold it. And it will last for millions of years. Yet when it is finally spent, the Word of God will live on.

Tear it apart into a thousand pages—and each will bring life. Bury it beneath tradition, ignorance, and brutal attack— and it will spring back to life. Try to contain it inside government or church restrictions—and one copy will escape and cause the Protestant Reformation. It is alive!

God's Word lives. And in order for us to live spiritually, we must come into contact with that Word. If you are spiritually lifeless, lethargic, and listless, it is because you are out of contact with the living Word. Contact it, come back to it, and it will give you new life. It is the road back to God.

GOD'S WORD CUTS

God's Word cuts superlatively; it is "sharper than any double-edged sword." The word used for "sharp" indicates something that cuts, and means comparatively more cutting. The two edges translate a term which means literally a "two-mouthed sword," as if both edges could bite through anything. Obviously, a sword with two edges cuts more, cuts both ways, cuts quickly. The word "sword" indicates the shorter, dagger-like sword worn by the Roman soldier for quick action. It is "the sword of the Spirit which is the word of God" (Eph. 6:17).

The smallest cutting devices yet made by man are glass micropipette tubes used in intercellular work on living cells. These glass knives are sixty-five hundred times thinner than the human hair. Yet there is something that can cut much finer. It is the Word of God. It can slice through the deepest evasions and finest distinctions of the deceptive human heart.

In another modern comparison, the finest cut ever made was reported in June 1983 at the Lawrence Livermore Laboratory in California. A special optical turning machine sliced a human hair three thousand times lengthwise. That's cutting it thin! But the Word of God is able to make cutting distinctions far finer than that. It is able to make the distinctions and incisions that bring us back to God.

At the point of sin, the Word of God must cut and kill before it can heal and make well—before there can be spiritual life. His living Word must be put to the throat of every sinful tendency, habit, and thought, and all must be sacrificed to the cutting edge of the Word. The Book is water to the fire of sin, antidote to the poison of sin, light to the darkness of sin, a key to the lock of sin. But it must first kill.

God's Word cuts thoroughly: "It penetrates even to dividing soul and spirit, joints and marrow." This is how the Word of God operates when we truly come into contact with its cutting power. It penetrates deeply; it strikes through to the very dividing line between the human soul and spirit. How often do we encounter a stubborn person and ask ourselves, *How can I get through to that person?* Only the Word has that capacity.

Understand what the word "separate" means. It means that the Word of God analyzes, lays bare, and reveals in their true nature all the powers of man. It separates the material from the immaterial, the spiritual from the animal parts of humans. It cuts through until it reveals that we are more than animals that eat, sleep, breed, and fight for territory. It does this by separating the spirit from the soul.

The human spirit is that which God placed in me; it is the point of contact with God. It retains the image of God and is breathed into me by God. The spirit makes me more than an animal.

The human soul, in comparison, is the seat of all my emotions, thoughts, feelings, desires, fixations, and inclinations. When it is cut off from the spirit, it is in chaos, lost, withered—a powerless plaything in the hands of material and demonic influence. When the Word of God comes, it cuts apart soul and spirit. It says, "Gregory, you were made to be more than a chaos of energies and passions." It lays bare and exposes the inside of me in a delicate spiritual surgery. That the Word of God separates between the joints and the marrow simply means that there is nothing inside of a person's real life that the Word of God does not show up in its true nature. No part of human nature is untouched. The very innermost part of my life is cleaved in twain by this mighty sword.

There is now hardly a place in the human body that surgeons can't penetrate with their arsenal of scalpels and lasers. Lasers can now cut away cataracts, remove brain tumors, and may soon effectively remove cholesterol deposits in coronary arteries. Now there is even an "excimer laser" that will allow exquisitely precise surgery through holes so small they will not need stitches. A special scalpel with a microwave device on it can heat tissue, clot blood at the moment of an incision, and allow incredible precision. Human technology is at an all-time high in its ability to cut, separate, and heal.

But it cannot compare with the divine technology that has always been here. More than any laser, the Book of God penetrates your life. Let it cut out of you that which does not belong to the will of God. There is no spiritual healing without such cutting. Let it cut specifically. If you covet, let its passages about covetousness cut you. If you lust, let its warnings about lust lacerate you. If you are angry, let its exposure of anger penetrate you. But as it cuts, feel it also healing you.

GOD'S WORD EXPOSES

God's Word exposes us personally: "It judges the thoughts and attitudes of the heart" (Heb 4:12). This Word of God sifts and scrutinizes both the emotions and the rational thoughts of our lives. It sifts every impulse, every secret thought, each desire, and all purposes. It does this by getting through to the human heart.

The Book of Hebrews warns us about the importance of the heart. We are told we must not harden the heart (3:8), for it tends to stray (3:10). God must write His law upon our hearts (8:10). We must draw near to God with a sincere heart (10:22) and can do that with a heart strengthened only by His grace (13:9).

As president of our state denomination I got to vote on some things I did not understand. Recently I was one of a group who voted to authorize a Baptist hospital to purchase a magnetic resonance imaging scanner, called an MRI. This instrument uses an electromagnet, radio waves, and a computer to penetrate the human body. Teeth and bones do not appear, enabling physicians to see tissue that otherwise would be obscured. Lives that would have been lost in the last decade are now saved because of this instrument that sees through the human body. If the author of Hebrews had had such an illustration at hand, he surely would have used it.

100

This modern machine can see through bone. But only the Word of God can see into the human spiritual mystery and expose all that is there. I lay my life under its energy and it reveals me to myself.

God's Word also exposes universally: "Nothing in all creation is hidden from God's sight" (Heb. 4:13a). Human technology has produced an optical satellite with the capacity to detect objects as small as seven inches across from a distance of two hundred miles above the earth's surface. Technologists also have perfected listening devices smaller than a postage stamp which can carry human conversations more than a block away to a listening post. The smallest video camera is now one and a half inches square and one inch thick. We have an amazing variety of devices to hear and to see where we could neither hear nor see before.

But these modern feats of technology cannot compare to the searching power of the Word of God. No created thing—nothing—will escape its search. No archangel, seraph, demon, or any other things that exist anywhere will escape the scrutinizing power of the Word of God. It will search and cut until all is discovered.

That is why the writer of Hebrews goes on to say positively that God's Word exposes powerfully: "Everything is uncovered and laid bare before the eyes of him to whom we must give account" (4:13b). In the presence of His word, everything is stripped of every disguise that conceals its true nature. We are experts at wearing masks, disguises, coverups. Stand under the power of this Word; let it cut, and all masks fall off.

There is a most interesting expression in the words "laid bare." Some suggest that it is the very word used to describe a Roman wrestler who grabbed his opponent by the neck and held his head back in full view. Others understand the word as a defeat which leaves its victim prostrate on the ground before the vanquished. Whichever interpretation is used, it simply means that the Word of God will conquer us all under the eyes of God Himself.

To know life we must submit and be laid bare, and let ourselves be saturated by that Word. We must let it cut, penetrate, expose, and give the only healing that is healing indeed. The following story show how God's Word affected one exemplary Christian life:

> Known primarily as an educator, Frank Gaebelein was the founding headmaster at the Stony Brook School, a Christian college preparatory school on Long Island, which has become a prototype. He held the post for 41 years and considered his work there his most important accomplishment.
>
> When once asked what he wished to pass on to the next generation of Christians, Gaebelein replied: "Maintain at all costs a daily time of scripture reading and prayer. As I look back, I see that the most formative influence in my life and thought has been my daily contact with scripture over 60 years."

Gretchen Gaebelein Hull, "Character Before Career,"
Christianity Today, quoted in Bob Benson and
Michael W. Benson,
Disciplines for the Inner Life
(Nashville: Generoux/Nelson, 1989), p. 54

Whatever the cost, the way back to God passes through daily contact with His Word.

The Lord is my light and my salvation—
  whom shall I fear?
The Lord is the stronghold of my life—
  of whom shall I be afraid?
When evil men advance against me
  to devour my flesh,
when my enemies and my foes attack me
  they stumble and fall.
Though an army besiege me,
  my heart will not fear;
though war break out against me,
  even then will I be confident.

One thing I ask of the Lord,
  this is what I seek:
that I may dwell in the house of the Lord
  all the days of my life,
to gaze upon the beauty of the Lord
  and to seek him in his temple.
For in the day of trouble
  he will keep me safe in his dwelling;
he will hide me in the shelter of his tabernacle
  and set me high upon a rock.
Then my head will be exalted
  above the enemies who surround me;
at his tabernacle will I sacrifice with shouts of joy;
  I will sing and make music to the Lord.

Psalm 27:1–6

10

Fear and Faith

Marjorie Goff was thirty-one when she stepped inside and closed the door of her small apartment in 1949. She did not leave her home again until she was sixty-one. She did go out one time in 1960 to visit her family. Two years later, she left again to have an operation. And in 1976, when the friend who shared her apartment was dying with cancer and wanted ice cream, Marjorie went out to get her some. She might still be there in her lonely apartment if it were not for a social worker who found her and helped her back out into the world!

"Extreme case," you say? Perhaps. But agoraphobia does afflict one in twenty Americans. It is literally fear of fear. An agoraphobiac is terrified by the possibility of a panic attack in an open place away from home. One woman suffered so acutely from agoraphobia that she literally could not be out of sight of her home. She walked backward out of her front door to pick up her morning paper in order never to lose sight of her house.

It might not always be this severe. But one in nine adults harbors some kind of phobia, making fear the number-one mental health problem for women, and the number-two problem for men, behind drug and alcohol abuse. It may well be that such abuse simply masks fear. There are phobias of shopping malls, freeways, and suspension bridges. In fact, one young truck driver was so afraid of the Chesapeake Bay Bridge that he could cross it only in the trunk of his car while his wife drove. A Los Angeles insurance executive is so fearful of driving on freeways that he holds tightly onto the roof of his car with one hand while he steers with the other. A San Francisco man who loved airplanes had logged 150,000 miles in the air when he encountered some turbulence in a 747. In a cold-sweat panic he quit flying—a problem for this thirty-seven-year-old man whose job depended on travel.

At least seventy-five phobias have been given technical names. Ailurophobia is the fear of cats. Astrophobia is the fear of lightning. Trichophobia is the fear of hair. One of the most unusual phobias is "triskaidekaphobia," fear of the number thirteen; it costs American business a billion dollars a year in absenteeism, cancellations, and reduced business on the thirteenth of the month. So deep is the fear of the number thirteen that in Paris a professional fourteenth guest can be hired to round out an otherwise ill-fated thirteen-person dinner.

You may say, "None of that is my problem." But remember that phobias are very personalized. While your friend's fear of spiders sends you into gales of laughter, your own fear of water seems perfectly sane, totally rational, and completely prudent. The fact of the matter is that your fear is real to you, whatever it may be.

The writer of the twenty-seventh psalm faced and conquered real fear. At some point in the midst of his trouble, the psalmist felt the pressing need to get back to God. "One thing I ask of the Lord, this is what I seek: that I may dwell in the house of the Lord all the days of my life" (27:4). This psalm is the testimony that a courageous king gave before the assembly of God's people. These are the words of an intrepid, invincible hero who has faced fear frequently and conquered because of faith. The objects of his fears were real, not imaginary. Vicious

106

enemies attacked him with words and weapons. Yet he found that faith elevated him above that which he feared. When communion with God dominates your life, faith is the antidote to fear. If you are in the grip of fear, come back to God.

OVERCOMING FEAR BY FAITH

Faith overcomes fear when God is first. The first words of this psalm form an expression of faith, "The Lord is my light and my salvation." Only after that affirmation of faith do you find the word "fear." The name of God is first before fear. This is as practical as waking up in the morning. Your first conscious thought will either be of faith or fear, belief or unbelief. The psalmist greeted the day with the name of God. Because of that, fear was shouted down by faith.

But this faith can't be vague or ambiguous. The faith that overcomes fear has solid content. The psalmist experiences God as light, victory, and stronghold. God as light overcomes fear because He alone pushes back every form of darkness. The psalmist had known the choking fear of nighttime military campaigns. He had known human enemies lurking somewhere behind a rock in the Judean desert. In such moments God was his light. He confessed elsewhere, "Indeed, the darkness shall not hide from You, But the night shines as the day; The darkness and the light are both alike to you" (139:12, NKJV).

Many still fear literal darkness; bad things do happen in the dark. Worse than physical darkness, though, are those things that belong to spiritual midnights—temptation and trouble. In all of it fear is finished when we confess, "God is my light."

Hughes Aircraft Corporation invented a small seven-and-one-fourth-pound instrument called "Probeye." It can see in the dark by detecting invisible, infrared radiation from a human body. Such technology enables humans to see in the dark what they could not see before. But all of us need something more than a "Probeye" in the spiritual darknesses that threaten us. This "something more" is Jehovah, who sheds the light that dispels darkness and shows the way out.

Further, the psalmist confesses that God is our salvation. On the safe side of trouble it is clear that He rescued us. God is also our stronghold, our refuge and bulwark. In the face of everything that gives terror, He is a place of safety. The faith that overcomes fear begins with the stalwart confession: "Jehovah is my light, salvation, and stronghold." Fear shrinks in the face of such an assault.

When this confession is an exclusive dependence upon God, it vanquishes fear. The psalmist means that he has stopped depending on any other human being to show him the way out, to rescue him, or to be a fortress for him. Nor does he ultimately depend on his own cleverness or personality. Against everything he fears, it's as though the psalmist cries, "God and God alone." By definition, if God is worthy of trust, He is worthy of *exclusive* trust.

These three words become a triple shield: light, salvation, stronghold. The world's most protected person is the president of the United States. He travels in an armored limousine, uses a bulletproof lectern, meets only guests screened by metal detectors, takes along his own food and water on the road, and lives in the White House surrounded by ground-to-air missiles to protect him in an air attack. Yet past attacks on ten presidents left four of them dead. All of the technology that humans can advance to protect an individual cannot ultimately protect. Only God is ultimately light, salvation, and fortress.

Faith overcomes fear when it is personal. The psalmist uses five first-person pronouns in verse 1. You cannot divorce the word "personal" from his faith. The psalmist did not overcome fear through understanding Old Testament theology. He did not just explain the theological concepts of light, salvation, and refuge. There may be more than half a million theological tomes and related materials in a nearby seminary library. But all of them together will not give you an ounce of courage in the face of fear unless your relationship to God is personal.

The psalmist did not recall that God had rescued Abraham, Isaac, and Jacob centuries before. Instead, he had the *personal* experience of God as rescuer. The faith that overcomes fear is the faith that moves from second-hand knowledge to first-hand experience, just as there is a great difference between reading the definition of "osculation" in a dictionary—and experiencing a kiss.

John R. Mott was a great Christian layman who led a world movement for modern missions. In his early university years he began to have doubts about the effectiveness of prayer. He could not see how it changed people or events outside the person who prayed. To deal with his doubts, he read forty-three books on prayer, but they did not deal with his doubts. He stopped reading, gave up his discussions, and began to pray. That's when he discovered the truth of the scripture, "The prayer of a righteous man is powerful and effective." The faith that overcomes fear is personal faith. Do you have that faith?

For that matter, it is personal faith that saves you eternally. Personal faith is the dividing line between those who practice religion and those who experience God.

Next, faith overcomes fear when we remember past experience. When faith has faced down fear in the past, you have an experience that heartens and encourages you for the future. If you have any personal faith, it has overcome some kind of fear in the past. The psalmist remembered definite past experiences when the wicked came against him—people who attacked him with intense personal ill will. They came against him to "eat up his flesh." This is a figure of speech meaning vicious language, to destroy one with words. The psalmist had experienced such vicious personal attack that he compares it to the assault of ravenous animals. Yet what became of it? "They stumbled and fell." Because of faith the worst did not happen. Is that not true with you? What has happened to most of the worst things you imagined? They did not happen.

We tend to forget today that in his early ministry Billy Graham was the object of scathing verbal attack from the press and the religious community. After his six-week crusade in Atlanta in 1950, the *Atlanta Constitution* published two photographs side by side on the front page. One was Billy Graham smiling and leaving town, and the other was ushers at the crusade holding huge money bags. Even when he gave away his offerings to local Christian causes, he was savaged by the press. Fundamentalist religious leaders like John Rice even attacked him from inside the church. But Graham chose to leave his attackers to God. When you see the mature, poised, courageous preacher today you can know that all that poise is based on past experiences of God's rescue in the midst of attack.

Bank on it: Faith will enable you to overcome fear today. And fear overcome today will give you more faith for tomorrow. The psalmist confessed his assurance for the future in verse 3: "Though an army besiege me, my heart will not fear; though war break out against me, even then will I be confident."

SINGLENESS OF DESIRE

Are you a "one-thing" person? The future fearlessness of your faith will rest on the singleness of your desire. The psalmist could affirm the "one thing have I desired of the Lord" (v. 4, KJV). People who give themselves to one thing always fascinate me. J. Hart Rosdail of Elmhurst, Illinois, gave himself to visiting all 221 countries and territories in the world. He visited all but two. He was a one-thing person. Beginning in 1950, Francis Johnson of Darwin, Minnesota, dedicated himself to collecting the largest ball of string: eleven feet in diameter and weighing five tons. Marva Drew of Waterloo, Iowa, between 1968 and 1974 typed the numbers one to one million in words on a manual typewriter. She used 2,473 pages. When asked why, she said, "I love to type."

These are preposterous examples of people obsessed with one thing. Many would wonder about the appropriateness of their obsessions. The psalmist, however, could speak of a single obsession that filled his own heart. When he looked to the past and into the future this one thing filled his perspective—and that perspective led him to strive for intense communion with and contemplation of God.

The psalmist makes one of the most single-minded statements to be found anywhere in Scripture when he writes: "that I may dwell in the house of the Lord all the days of my life." He habitually longs to be in Jehovah's house, to be in close communication with Him both physically and spiritually. But he was often under attack and had to flee far from the tabernacle or tent that housed the visible presence of the unseen God. So he envied those servants of the tabernacle who perpetually lived in its very physical presence. Likewise, the same faith that overcomes fear today is a faith that longs to be in the congregation of God's people where they gather together in His presence. The faith of a spiritual isolationist has difficulty overcoming fear. But the faith that feeds on the gathering of God's people locally and physically in the congregation is the faith that can face down fear.

Paul Johnson is a British author and professor. One Sunday morning he woke up with burning anger after a prominent man had publicly criticized him unfairly on an important issue. Johnson intended to respond with a vicious response. But it was Sunday morning, so first he went to church. There he measured himself by the yardstick of eternity. His entire perspective changed. His fear of criticism was assuaged in the white light of God's Word and in the fellowship of the church.

But there is a larger dimension to our gathering into a local congregation. Fearless faith practices the contemplation of God. And what in the world do you do at church to meet

God? The psalmist desires "to behold the beauty of the Lord" (v. 4, KJV). He wants to gaze at God. He refers many times to his yearning for a clinging, lingering, entranced gaze at God. "As for me, I will see Your face in righteousness; I shall be satisfied when I awake in Your likeness" (Ps. 17:15, NKJV). How does the psalmist do this? He looks beyond the ritual, the ceremony, the words, and the music to the living God. He contemplates everything in the gathering of the congregation and the service of worship for what it tells us about God. Even when he is away, he practices gazing at and contemplating God.

The faith that faces down fear practices this singular desire—to meet God personally in the place of worship. You should not come to the place of worship to escape involvement in a fearful world, but because the place of worship makes you equal to involvement in a fearful world.

The Christian today faces the temptation to spiritualize this confession. In the Old Testament, David wanted to be at the tabernacle in order to meet God. In the New Testament we are not tied to a single place to commune with God. But this still does not devalue the necessity of a singular desire to be with God's people in God's house. This does not mean that there is a one-to-one correspondence between being at God's house and facing your fear. A man in the United Church of Christ of Columbia, Illinois, attended church for three thousand consecutive Sundays over a period of more than fifty-seven years. I do not know whether he faced fear better than others. But I do know that among those whose faith is personal, there is a longing to gaze at God in the sanctuary of His people. And out of that experience of coming together, God's people draw the resources of faith to face down fear.

REALIZING GOD'S PROTECTION

What does God do for the person who has personal faith and seeks only to commune with God in the midst of His people? At some times God hides that person in days of fear and at

112

other times, God elevates that person above the things which threaten.

Personal faith does give a hiding place, a retreat in fearful times. The psalmist uses a series of words which mean a house, a tabernacle, a tent, an asylum, a sanctuary—places in which he sees himself as God's protected guest. Behind this is the great biblical custom of absolute right of protection by one's host. To this day among Bedouins in the desert, to be in the tent of a host, to break bread with him, is to enjoy his absolute protection. It is the same heartening, encouraging word found in Psalm 23:5: "You prepare a table before me in the presence of my enemies." Right there in the presence of hostile people, the psalmist finds a retreat in communion with God. This does not speak of escape from fear, but of the courage to endure fear and triumph.

Studdert Kennedy, the great World War I chaplain, used to tell of listening to two frightened soldiers during a heavy bombardment of their trench. Between the howling of the shells and the immense crashings, he heard a sergeant cursing vividly while a man next to him was despairing and shivering and praying for safety. He said the latter kind of praying was the more disgusting of the two. Studdert Kennedy asked himself what, then, was prayer that was not contemptible, or selfish, or useless? He concluded that true prayer is not that which asks for permission to survive but for courage to endure.

You must have a hiding place, a place to come apart— or you will literally come apart. Jesus told His disciples after rigorous ministry in the face of opposition and crowds, "Come aside by yourselves to a deserted place and rest a while" (Mark 6:31).

Personal faith protects us by elevating us above the difficulties: "He shall set me high upon a rock. And now my head shall be lifted up above my enemies . . ." (Ps. 27:5–6, NKJV). Here the psalmist describes a different reality. He finds himself elevated upon a prominent rock, standing out starkly against the landscape. Far beneath are the same enemies he described in verse 2. The causes for fear are still very real; but he now finds himself far above them. He is in a sheltering asylum on a hill where Jehovah guards him from trouble and makes him inaccessible to dangers far beneath him. It is a sense of being above the fray, unafraid because of faith.

This image was played out for me in real life when several years ago, Linda, Grant, Garrett, and I were driving through the northern coast of South Wales near Cardigan. We spent the night at a remote cottage toward the end of the road by the sea. Climbing over a stile in the fence, we walked through a pasture of sea grass that was as calm as a sheep fold. But suddenly we found ourselves standing on the edge of a mighty gorge. It had been eaten out by the crashing of gigantic waves that roared into Cardigan Bay, crumbling the rocky cliff and exploding in a mighty roar of foam and water hundreds of feet below us. Anxiously watching the boys stand near the edge of the great gorge, I could scarcely remember a stranger contrast in my life—a calm meadow behind us, the wrath of a furious sea beneath us. We stood between the two, strangely safe and calm on top of that rock. David experienced that same exhilaration as he heard the crash of hostility around him while knowing that he was elevated far above it in Jehovah.

We know it far better in the promise of God through Christ Jesus: "God raised us up with Christ and seated us with him in the heavenly realms in Christ Jesus" (Eph. 2:6). When you come back to God, you can get on top of your fears.

Part III

Staying with God

For this reason he had to be made like his brothers in every way, in order that he might become a merciful and faithful high priest in service to God, and that he might make atonement for the sins of the people. Because he himself suffered when he was tempted, he is able to help those who are being tempted.

For we do not have a high priest who is unable to sympathize with our weaknesses, but we have one who has been tempted in every way, just as we are—yet was without sin. Let us then approach the throne of grace with confidence, so that we may receive mercy and find grace to help us in our time of need.

Hebrews 2:17–18; 4:15–16

11

The Lord Jesus: A Friend in Temptation

Sometimes going it alone is going nowhere. If you name a handicap, a medical condition, or a life-disrupting situation, you'll probably find a support group ready to help people with that problem. There are an estimated half-million support groups in the United States serving upward of fifteen million people. Some of these are highly structured. Others are informal. Some meet on a regular basis—once a week, once a month. Others do not have regular meetings, but provide support in other ways. However they differ, they share a common goal. They bring together people of similar experiences who, by sharing, find strength and support from one another.

There are groups for widespread illnesses such as cancer and heart disease. There are groups for relatively unknown conditions such as sarcoidosis, a chronic skin disease. Candlelighters is a group for parents of children with leukemia. Pil-Anon offers aid to families of persons addicted to mood-altering drugs. There are support groups for parents who lose a child, and groups for people with brain injuries, genetic defects, chronic metabolic diseases, burns, and diabetes.

The names of these groups are sometimes symbolic. Mended Hearts is the group for those with heart surgery. The Phoenix Society is for recovering burn victims. For those who lose a baby there is Empty Cradle. Then there's the grandparent of all American self-help organizations, Alcoholics Anonymous.

These groups indicate that going it alone is often going nowhere. When life's crises strike, most of us seek help from someone with similar experience. But where do we ultimately go when faced with spiritual crisis? Where do we go when temptation beckons? We may confess temptation to one another; but that is not enough. We need the One who has the world's most extensive experience with temptation. The Hebrew letter repeatedly emphasizes the identity and sympathy of the Lord Jesus with you in temptation. He cannot identify with you in sin. That is foreign to Him; He has no experience of sin except suddenly bearing it on the cross. But He has the most extensive experience of temptation anyone ever had.

When we come back to God, we may believe that nothing will ever lure us away from His presence again. But that is not always the case. Temptation is an integral part of our earthly life. When it whispers to us, two passages in Hebrews 2 and 4 indicate three ways Jesus helps us turn our backs to the devil—and stay with God.

Jesus helps us do this by His identification with us, His sympathy for us, and His provision for us in temptation. Jesus Christ is our best friend in temptation. We have access to Him if we know Him. Take advantage of that access for help. Doing so is the assurance that you will stay after you come back to God.

UNDERSTANDING CHRIST'S
IDENTIFICATION WITH US

Jesus identifies with us in a broader sense than in just our temptations. He identifies with the entire situation of human life. "He had to be made like his brothers in every way . . ."

118

(Heb. 2:17). Our salvation is because of His identification with us. To build a bridge to God and to pay for sin, He had to identify with us. He was bound, obligated, felt the necessity, was under the imperative to identify with us in every way. This does not mean that He had to identify with us against His own will. It does mean that once He undertook the task to be Savior, this identification with us was an obligation that went along with the task.

It means that He could never have helped us from remoteness, aloofness, or isolation. His involvement is illustrated by the story of an ancient Roman general who had legions upon legions at his command. Among his officers was his own son, who already bore the signs of greatness. When the battle was about to be fought, his son urged a certain strategy. "Do this," he said. "Advance in this way. We shall have success, and it will only cost five thousand men." The old general turned solemnly to his son and put the quiet question: "Will you be one of the five thousand?" When Jesus Christ pondered the salvation of humans, he did not do it from behind the lines, counting the casualties of others in a comfortable heavenly headquarters. When the Father asked if He would be one of them, fighting the war with them, He said, "I delight to do your will, Lord."

There was not only a necessity in this identification, but also a totality—"in every way." Not a single ingredient was left out in His identification with our situation. He identifies with us in a genuine struggle to seek, find, and do the will of God. Luke 2:52 tells us that Jesus "grew." The word itself speaks of an extension by blows, as a blacksmith stretches metal with hammers. It also refers to a scout hacking his way through underbrush in advance of an army. Christ struggled, wrestled—and stood in solidarity with us. Hebrews 5:8 tells us that "he learned obedience from what he suffered."

There is no aspect of your life with which He cannot identify. What are your circumstances? Did you come from obscurity? He came from Nazareth. Did you come from a humble background? He came from peasant parents. Do you have limited education? He had very little formal training outside His home. Have you ever faced rejection? He knew it unabated—His own home town, religious leaders, the general population, government—all rejected Him. Have you been misunderstood? No one has ever been as misjudged as He. Has life been awfully unfair to you? The Cross was the greatest injustice of history. Have you been betrayed by a friend? He was betrayed by His own disciple. Have you felt abandoned? He cried out, "My God, My God, why have You forsaken Me?" (Mark 15:34, NKJV).

Have you had problems with your family? Look at His relationships. His own mother, brothers, and sisters did not understand Him. Have you ever lost someone you loved? He loved and lost Lazarus—and wept. Have you ever suffered the extreme pain of unrequited love—have you loved someone who did not love you in return? Love flowed out of His mouth, streamed from His eyes, reached out from His heart—only to be spurned.

Look at His physical life. He knew fatigue, tiredness, lack of accommodation, absence of food. He entered into all of the sordid, earthly qualities of life as a struggle for existence.

Let no one say, "He does not understand me. As the glorified prince of heaven, he cannot understand my situation." No! Where we have felt a pound of humanity He has lifted a ton. Where we have swallowed a drop, He has swallowed an ocean. You can never turn your face toward heaven only to hear Him say, "I do not understand."

You would think that it would have been enough for Him to identify with the human situation, that subjecting Himself to the mere struggle would seem like enough. But He descended further than that. He identifies with us in temptation: "Because he himself suffered when he was tempted . . ." (2:18), "tempted in every way, just as we are" (4:15). The emphasis rests on the reality of His temptation. It was no mock battle, no shadowboxing, no charade. The stress falls on the duration of His temptations. Throughout His life He faced them. In the wilderness, in the suggestion of Peter, in the request of His own family to abandon His mission, and in the final great temptation in Gethsemane.

He faced temptation in the same categories we face it. But beyond that, He faced an additional peculiar sort of temptation because of His mission. He faced the constant temptation to turn away from it, to follow an easier path. In Gethsemane God's will was clearly not what He wanted. In the strongest language, He contrasted His personal will with that of the Father: "Nevertheless, not my will, but thine, be done" (Luke 22:42, KJV; see also Matt. 26:39 and Mark 14:36). In John 5:30 he said, "I seek not to please myself but him who sent me" and in John 6:38, "I have come down from heaven not to do my will but to do the will of him who sent me." Romans 15:3 tells us that "even Christ did not please himself."

Jesus Christ was continually engaged in a struggle between His will and the will of the Father, the duration and extent of which are beyond our ability to know or understand.

But beyond the reality and the extent of Christ's temptation, there was also the intensity of temptation to become alienated from God in His world. Jesus was like someone with perfect pitch always having to listen to terrible disharmony. He was like someone with a perfect eye for art having to view a terrible mixture of the wrong colors. Because of this, only Jesus could really know what temptation is.

In the spiritual realm, Jesus was like a man who feels in his body the warning of pain, seeks medical advice, and receives remedial treatment. The rest of us are like those who do not recognize sickness, who conceal and deny it until the illness is ready to leap out like an enemy to overwhelm us when we least expect it. Jesus was constantly aware of the symptoms of temptation and constantly battling them. We who have been so often defeated by temptation are so deafened, blinded, anesthetized, and insensitive that we do not even feel a fraction of the temptation that Jesus felt.

There was an exception in Jesus' temptation, though: "yet was without sin" (4:15). Second Corinthians 5:21 states He "had no sin." First Peter 2:22 affirms "He committed no sin." He could ask, "Which of you convicts me of sin?" and no one in history could lay a finger on Him. How close to sinning did Jesus ever get? In a desperately long battle a soldier may yearn with every muscle in his weary body to gain the relief of desertion; but it is possible for him at the same time never to deviate a hair's breadth from the "set" of his loyalty to his country's cause. There were moments when Jesus yearned to desert, but He set His will to do the Father's will above all else.

Such identification shocks us and helps us. Beulah Lund, a fifty-year-old mother of four from Deer Park, Washington, found that out in her own way. Beulah is married to a successful contractor and lives in a spacious farmhouse set on 171 acres twenty-two miles north of Spokane. When she visited the nation's capital she was haunted by the scores of street people she saw. The image so haunted her that she told her husband of thirty-two years that she was going to go back and live like a street person in order to understand their world.

She flew from Seattle to Washington, D.C. and took a crash course on street survival from a shelter worker; then the ordeal started immediately. One day she trudged the streets for six hours just looking for a drink of water. As darkness came she could not find the shelter. And when she did find it, the shelter was dirty, vulgar, and drug-ridden. During one of the nine nights she spent in the shelter, her life was threatened with a pair of scissors at her throat. She started to live on the streets, eating the remains of sandwiches and pasta that secretaries threw away on their lunch hours. She did her laundry in public fountains and dried it on the spotlights pointed at the Washington Monument. Incoherent, with high fever and strep throat, she went home—but returned four days later to finish her effort at identification.

When she finally returned home, she began to lecture publicly on the problems of street people. She is now an effective advocate for the homeless because of her personal identification with them. (*People Weekly*, 16 February 1987, pp. 32–34)

In much the same sense, the Lord Jesus Christ did what Beulah Lund did in order to return home as an effective advocate. He clothed Himself like us, slept where we sleep, ate what we eat, faced the cold nights of our own human existence— and overcame it all. You may turn to Him in any temptation as the One who knows. He left heaven to become a street person on earth.

ACCEPTING CHRIST'S COMPASSION

Christ's identity with us extends as compassion for us in our temptation. In Hebrews 2:17, He is described as a "merciful and faithful high priest." We can understand the word "priest" better if we take it literally. The Latin word for priest is *pontifex*. It means a "bridge builder." Jesus is our faithful bridge builder. In the Old Testament the high priest had a very specialized function on one significant day, recorded in Leviticus 16. That was the Day of Atonement. On that day the high priest went into God's presence to offer a collective sacrifice for the sins of all the people. Everyone depended upon his being a faithful bridge builder between God and man.

Yet this high priest often did not know every member of the congregation. He was a remote and aristocratic figure. While he performed a function of eternal significance, he often did not know those for whom he performed it. He could have no personal compassion for them. He was building a bridge to God but did not know those who would pass over it.

In contrast, our high priest—Jesus—is merciful. In relationship to each tempted person He feels pity and compassion. The word suggests a feeling of mercy for those who are in a wretched situation. So often the Old Testament priests failed at the point of mercy. During the time of Jesus, there were

twenty-eight high priests in 107 years. They were cruel, inso-
lent, and greedy. In the days of Caiaphas, worshipers were run
out of the temple area by priests wielding sticks when it got
too crowded. People longed for someone to build a bridge to
God who felt compassion for them.

Jesus is faithful as well as merciful. We can trust Him
with absolute confidence. In all of His relationships to us, He
is always the same. His compassion is based on His position
as merciful and faithful high priest, and bridge builder. The
Simon and Garfunkel song "Bridge Over Troubled Water" was
really not a religious song. But it struck a chord in the hearts
of a generation that desperately wanted somebody to care and
to bridge trouble. All of us need a bridge builder when we are
struggling with temptation.

Christ's compassion for us also comes from His sympathy: "We do not have a high priest who is unable to sympathize
with our weaknesses . . ." (Heb. 4:15). This statement antici-
pates an objection. For example, one might wonder, *How can
Jesus Christ, the Son of God enthroned in glory at the right
hand of the Father, have sympathy with the weaknesses of my
little life? How can a powerful king in a palace sympathize with
the weakness of a sick, poor man?*

This passage affirms that our Lord has habitual sympathy. The word does not mean the compassion of one who
regards sympathy from without. It refers to One who enters
into someone else's suffering and makes it His own. His feeling toward us is not pity; it is not feeling *for* us, but feeling
with us. He has what we might call "fellow-feelings." He is
touched. He shares our infirmity, our feeble flesh. This does
not say that He has only sympathy with our heroic moments,
our great deeds, our noble sacrifices. He also feels with us
our abject weaknesses.

Is there a man who all the days of his life controls anger,
temper, and rage? Who fights it, disciplines it—and sometimes loses it? Our Lord feels the man's weakness, and has
compassion. Is there a woman who fights the fatigue that

124

comes from career and family and endless responsibility? Our Lord feels her weakness, and has compassion.

There is no one who can help me like someone who shares my experience. That's the enduring foundation of Alcoholics Anonymous, which was started in 1935 by two alcoholics: a doctor named Bob, and a stockbroker named Bill W. There are now more than fifty-three thousand AA groups worldwide with more than one million members.

Born in 1895, Bill W. was in a home torn apart by arguments. At age ten his parents divorced and Bill was left with his maternal grandparents. He became an obsessive over-compensator in every area of life. He did not take a drink until he was a twenty-two-year-old army officer stationed at New Bedford, Massachusetts. But right from the start, he was a black-out drinker. It ruined his career as a stock analyst and speculator and caused him to flunk his final exam at Brooklyn Law School. The 1929 stock market crash wrecked him financially and finished off what drinking had not already ruined. Then an old drinking friend, Ebby Thatcher, contacted him and told him of an experience with God that had changed his life. Out of the sympathy of someone who knew from the inside what he faced, Bill W.'s life began to change.

Bill W., in turn, contacted Dr. Bob, a desperate alcoholic who had tried to stop but could not. On June 10, 1935, Dr. Bob took his last drink. And that was the day Alcoholics Anonymous was born—born on the basis of people with the same experience sharing out of knowledge and compassion. No one can help anyone like someone who has been there.

Another example of this kind of sympathetic compassion is found in the story of Martha Morrison, a bright student who careened through the drug culture, starting at age twelve. Although she was an across-the-spectrum drug abuser, she graduated from the University of Arkansas and from medical school. Finally, after years of struggling with her addiction, she consented to go to the famous Ridgeview Institute in Smyrna, Georgia—where she tried to hang herself thirty-six hours after entering. In group therapy with others who had the same problem, she began to find wholeness. She met the grace of God. Now, at age thirty-one, she is the associate director of Ridgeview's highly regarded adolescent chemical-dependency unit, helping others with a sympathy from experience.

Jesus is not the founder of "Sinners Anonymous," because He never sinned. But He is the one who is full of mercy and compassion for those who resist temptation. He has walked where you walk. He knows the full force of your every temptation. He does not feel *for* you, he feels *with* you. When you are faced with temptation, do not consider Him a remote judge. Stop and consider: *Jesus Christ does not condone my sin. But He understands my weakness. He knows the fierce heat of temptation.*

With Jesus beside you, when you come back to God—you can stay.

On the last and greatest day of the Feast, Jesus stood and said in a loud voice, "If anyone is thirsty, let him come to me and drink. Whoever believes in me, as the Scripture has said, streams of living water will flow from within him." By this he meant the Spirit, whom those who believed in him were later to receive. Up to that time the Spirit had not been given, since Jesus had not yet been glorified.

John 7:37-39

On the last and greatest day of the Feast, Jesus stood
and said in a loud voice, "If anyone is thirsty, let him come
to me and drink. Whoever believes in me, as the Scripture
has said, streams of living water will flow from within him."
By this he meant the Spirit, whom those who believed in him
were later to receive. Up to that time the Spirit had not been
given, since Jesus had not yet been glorified.

John 7:37–39

12

Come and Drink

It is as if Americans had discovered water again. Restaurant patrons want water brought in a bottle so they can read the label. Something like fifty-nine varieties of bottled water are available today. For serious water drinkers to order water now demands the same discernment that used to be reserved for other beverages. A waiter may be asked, "Is this water imported or domestic? Is it natural (all from one source) or processed (mixed from several sources)? Is it still or effervescent? And if it's effervescent, is the carbonation natural or was it added artificially?

I'm not kidding! From Europe alone come such brands as Solare, Fiuggi, Spa, San Pelligrino, Apollinaris, and of course, Perrier, from Vergeze, France—the bottled-water champion. Recently the company doubled its operations to eight hundred million bottles per year. In the United States you can buy Mountain Valley Water, which has been bottled for 115 years in good old Hot Springs, Arkansas. All this attention makes it seem as if people were looking for something special in water. Perhaps they're looking for a meaning that water itself does not hold.

People in Jesus' generation could not be so selective

about the water they drank. To have water at all was a great gift of God. The last great feast of the year, the Feast of Tabernacles, celebrated God's gift of water to His people. It was on this occasion that Jesus made His great statement about water, describing living water flowing from within, the Holy Spirit residing in and presiding over the lives of His people.

This same living water is still there for us today when we come back to God—and stay. It swirls through us and around us, quenching us, energizing us, comforting us, inspiring us, and protecting us. It is the gift of life everlasting in God's presence.

CRYING OUT

Each year the Feast of Tabernacles in Jerusalem recreated the wilderness wanderings of the Hebrew people. On the streets, in the courts, and on the roofs people lived in arbors constructed of palms, myrtles, and olives. Looking up at night, they saw the stars through these booths and remembered the Exodus. The ceremonies of the week defy description. Seventy bulls were sacrificed for the seventy nations of the world. The temple trumpets sounded a triumphant blast twenty-one times. On the evening of the first day a huge candelabra was lit in the court of the women, and in the light of the torches men danced until the temple gates closed at night. The celebration of water dominated the whole week.

On each of the seven mornings of the feast, the multitude followed the priests to the pellucid pool of Siloam, fed by the sacred spring of Gihon southeast of the temple hill. There, with great ceremony, the white-robed priest filled a shining golden pitcher with the living, sparkling water of the spring as the people cried out from Isaiah with one voice, "With joy you will draw water from the wells of salvation." Then the masses of people—children wild-eyed with wonder, women rapturous with joy, old men with renewed vigor—all of them

130

proceeded back up to the temple, singing the six psalms which end with Psalm 118.

In their left hands the people carried twigs representing the journey of the Exodus and in their right hands they held fruits representing the land of promise. The silver trumpets blasted as they circled the altar, and then the real moment arrived. The priest ascended a ramp with the golden pitcher in hand and poured the water through a bright silver funnel until it landed, laughing and splashing, on the pavement below. The occasion was so filled with joy that one rabbi said those who had not seen it did not know what joy meant. If it rained during the feast, it was seen as a forecast of abundant rain and harvest. All of this was the setting of one of Jesus' greatest statements.

John 7:37 says, "On the last and greatest day of the Feast, Jesus stood and said in a loud voice. . . . " Some believe that the last day of the feast was a solemn Sabbath with no ceremony, and that the people were quiet and stilled as they kept the Sabbath around the great temple. Amid that quiet setting, Jesus stood up and cried out. Normally He taught from a seated position, but here His posture as well as His voice demanded attention. He cried out in the midst of the solemn Sabbath, His voice reverberating in the halls of the Jerusalem temple. Just as we are told Jesus "cried out" in the tomb of Lazarus, calling life out of death, with that same intensity He "cries out" into the lifeless religious ceremony in Jerusalem.

It was an electrifying interruption. The impact would be similar to someone standing up and crying out the same way in the public worship service of a large church. It would be like crying out at a presidential inauguration or a solemn graduation. It was an audacious, preempting, substitutionary act. Jesus cried out that He is the replacement for all empty ceremony; He is the substance of which all else is the shadow. He is the real of which all else is the symbol.

131

Many of us need to hear that cry. We come to religious ceremonies, we follow the order of service, we watch the pageantry, and hear the praises, but still we thirst. We are parched, and still not fulfilled.

Hearing the Invitation of Christ

Christ calls first for our recognition of need: "If anyone is thirsty. . . . " Jesus compared the intensity of higher spiritual needs with the intensity of lower physical needs. Before Jesus, the psalmist had cried, "My soul thirsteth for God, for the living God" (Ps. 42:2, KJV). And Jeremiah had cried out to his generation that they had "hewn themselves . . . broken cisterns" (Jer. 2:13, NKJV). In that day, people's lives leaked. They were like cracked containers, the water of life slowly seeping out of them. Jesus had proclaimed earlier, "Blessed are those who hunger and thirst for righteousness, for they will be filled" (Matt. 5:6).

Jesus' use of thirst in His appeal would surely touch a nerve in His desert-dwelling listeners. Today, we cannot imagine what thirst really meant to that generation. The Feast of Tabernacles took place in October, after the seemingly endless stretch of blistering desert days. The thirsty person of Jesus' day knew the torture of fine sand entering every pore of the skin, choking and blinding, and the scorching wind drying up the very marrow of the bones. A human can live a long time without food; but seventeen days is the world record without water. Experts say there are five stages of extreme physical thirst. First, there is a protest stage of disbelief and discomfort. Then the mouth feels as dry as cotton and the tongue sticks to the roof of the mouth. Next there comes the agony of the tongue shriveling into a knot; in agony, the victim tears at his clothes. Next the skin cracks from lack of water. And finally there's the writhing, convulsive end. This is the picture of extreme physical thirst.

But spiritual thirst can be just as real. And even worse, there are some so dead to life and to God that they are beyond spiritual thirst. They have drunk at the fetid, stagnant, foul wells of godless existence until there is no spiritual thirst left. For them life is only a long day's journey into night.

If they have not found the Source of living water, those who do feel a spiritual thirst try to fill it endlessly. They fill their thirst with money, but only want more. They fill it with sensuality, but one conquest only makes them want another. They fill it with ambition, but that is like drinking salt water. They fill it with the desire for power, but every little bit makes them jealous of those who have more. When you try to fill the God-shaped void in your life with conquests in the bedroom or the board room it only stokes inward fires with an intenser heat. It is the same thirst felt by a drug abuser who moves from amphetamines to marijuana to cocaine to crack to heroine, trying to douse the fire within him. If anyone has eyes to see he can witness a horde of people whose souls have shriveled with spiritual thirst.

What do you have to know to come to Jesus Christ? The only fitness required is the knowledge of your need. All you need to do is humbly admit, "Lord, I thirst." And hearing your whispered plea, Christ opens His arms: ". . . let him come to me and drink." He simply offers Himself. When we come back to God to stay, that is all we need.

The image of Jesus' invitation is one of comfort and refreshment. Remember the setting in the Feast of Tabernacles. The priest had ceremonially poured out water from a golden pitcher into a silver funnel for seven days. But despite the elaborate ritual, when the people drank, the ceremonial water quenched their thirst only temporarily. Those who drank from the waters of the ceremony would eventually be thirsty again. But Jesus gives an invitation away from a ceremony to a person, away from an outward rite to an inward reality.

The first meaning of this invitation is that Christ calls us away from the external, formal, and ritual in religion and calls us to Himself. "Everyone who drinks this water will be thirsty again, but whoever drinks the water I give him will never thirst" (John 4:13).

The whole of John's Gospel presents Jesus as the fulfillment of every religious ceremony and symbol. In chapter 1 He is the true lamb of God and the true ladder to heaven. In chapter 2, He is the real temple; in chapter 3, He is the real birth; in chapter 6, He is the real manna from heaven; in chapter 7, He is the true water from the rock; in chapter 8, He is the true light of the world; and finally, in chapter 19, He is the true passover lamb.

Christ professes to be the inexhaustible person, welcoming all of humanity in every generation; even then, there will be more than enough from this artesian well. Place these words on the lips of anyone else and see how ridiculous they sound. A pastor could never say this—I certainly know that! I pour myself out in preparation, preaching, visitation, counseling, and then in emptiness I must come back to the great Font. No Plato of philosophy, no Einstein of intellect, no politician, no academician, no sage or philosopher ever made this statement. But Christ can, and twenty centuries have proven its truth. The apostles drank from this Source in the first century; but at the end of their era the blessed Source was still brimful.

Justin Martyr and Irenaeus and thousands of other Christian martyrs drank of it in the second century, and they died saying it is still full. Origen and Clement and the great commentators of the third century drank; and when they laid down their pens, the well was still overflowing. Augustine and his generation drank in the fourth century and died crying out, "There is still more!" That well flowed through the Dark Ages, a river flowing through the night of superstition that chained Bibles in cathedrals. In the twelfth, thirteenth, and fourteenth centuries they came to drink—John Syclif, John Huss, Thomas Aquinas, and others, and they all cried out, "The longer it flows, the deeper it grows!" Then the great reformers and the thousands they brought to Christ all drank.

134

Luther gave the cup to Calvin, and cried, "John, it's still full!" Calvin passed the cup to Knox in Scotland, and cried, "The more you drink, John, the more there is!" Oliver Cromwell and the Puritans drank and John Smyth and the Separatists drank, and still, the further it went, the wider it would grow, and the deeper it would flow.

That river flowed through colonial America in great awakenings and it became a mighty wave that flowed over the Appalachians to the great revivals on the frontier. It flows right down to this very day. Will you drink?

THE RESOURCE FOR LIFE

Jesus, the Source of Life, promises to flow to and through the believer—and through us as sources to others. In order to say this, Jesus laid His hand on two great images from the old Testament—the water from the rock of the Exodus and the river from the temple in Ezekiel.

In the Old Testament Exodus, God provided water for His people by telling Moses to "smite the rock," and from that rock flowed water. The rabbis maintained that the rock followed after Israel in the wilderness. Paul said in 1 Corinthians 10:3–4, "They all . . . drank the same spiritual drink: for they drank of that spiritual rock that accompanied them, and that rock was Christ." The water came from a smitten rock. John adds in this passage that "Up to that time the Spirit had not been given, since Jesus had not yet been glorified" (v. 39).

It was in dying that Jesus, the great Living Stone, opened His side to give the water of life. "One of the soldiers pierced Jesus' side with a spear, bringing a sudden flow of blood and water" (John 19:34). There is water from the Rock! It is a great mystery that out of the death of Christ we find the water of life.

Less profound mystery also surrounds some of the water in our earthly life, especially the world's great rivers. High among the everlasting snows of the tallest Andes, a thin trickle of water suddenly bubbles forth and starts to trace a hesitant line on the face of the rock. It edges its way slowly down like a twisting sliver of light. More than thirty-six hundred miles later the Amazon empties into the Atlantic at 180,000 cubic meters per second, draining one-fifth of all the water that runs off the earth's surface. Sixty miles into the Atlantic it still purifies the salt water. Yet it began as a tiny trickle from a mysterious source.

The greatest mystery of all is the Nile. It begins in an unknown source more than eighty-five hundred feet up in the mountains of Burundi, and empties into the sea 4,154 miles later.

The water of life that flows from the side of Jesus Christ is more than a river of mystery; it is the water of life. From the smitten Rock of Ages, from the side of the wounded Christ, flow water and blood.

The other image on which Christ laid His hand was the mighty river from the temple in Ezekiel 47. The great prophet foresaw that from the temple in Jerusalem there would come a river that would flow to the Judean desert, into the Jordan, and on to the Dead Sea. The further it went, the deeper it would grow, and the wider it would flow, Ezekiel wrote. Jesus had claimed to replace the temple: "the temple he had spoken of was his body" (John 2:21). And in the last pages of Scripture we read of the river that flows "from the throne of God and of the Lamb" (Rev. 22:1).

But it is not enough that Jesus is the Source of life for others. The great meaning is that this Source enters the life of those who come to Christ—who come home to God, and stay. He who comes to the Rock becomes a rock. He who drinks from this Fountain becomes a fountain. This answers the promise of Isaiah: "You will be . . . like a spring whose waters never fail" (Isa. 58:11).

Jesus Christ pours Himself into us and we become fountains like Him. We become like the melting snows of the highlands, which pour themselves down into some great lake whose clear water reflects the blue sky above; we become

136

like the rivers that carry to the lowland valleys all of the glorious force of the snow-melted waters from the hills. The water of life empties itself into the great lake of Jesus Christ, but He then flows through the innermost being of all those who are His. In this way, the Christian life is lived as He meant it to be lived, showing these three characteristics:

1. The life of Christ through us is one of effortlessness—the waters flow. There is no effort about a river—it simply flows. What strain there is in the life of most of us! We pump ourselves up and whip ourselves into shape. But when we touch this soothing secret of Christ, life flows without a sense of strain to us or to others.

2. The life of Christ through us is one of abundance. The word "abundant" comes from the Latin *ab unda* which means "wave upon wave." Notice in John 7:38 that Christ said "streams of living water will flow from within him"—streams, plural. Not one, but many. There is more than enough living water for everything in your life. A stream of water for your home, a stream of water for your work, and another for your service to Christ.

3. The life of Christ within us is internal in its origin. It leaps forth from our innermost beings. We have an inward source that speaks to those around us of something divine. When I was a boy, I saw a fascinating exhibit at the famous Fort Worth, Texas rodeo. It was a faucet hanging on a string. Water came from it, but it was not connected to anything. It was, of course, a trick; a thin, transparent rod carried water up through the stream of water to the faucet. What appeared to be a secret source of water was really an optical illusion. But with Christ there is no illusion. There is only reality. He really is a Source fed from unseen reserves who pours His very life into us.

F. B. Meyer, the great Christian mystic of the late nineteenth and early twentieth century, told of a meeting of 150 of God's servants. They met with Meyer and Dr. Wilbur Chapman out in an old woods, on an Indian mound. One of the

137

Christians told of the way he had struggled up and out of his former discouragement. He had read in a secular newspaper an address which made it clear that one thing mattered in Christian living: "whether a man worked for God or whether he let God work through him." His whole life changed because of that simple but radical distinction. Meyer, Chapman, and all the others knelt down in the woods and prayed audibly, one after another, "Not henceforth for thee, O God, but Thou through me." The difference afterward was electrifying in life and fulfillment. (*Homiletic Review*, October 1899, 323)

Jesus offers to flow through you in a new dimension of Christian living. That is the way to stay back when you have come back to God.